Disney Films and Secret Messages
Race, Ethnicity, Gender and Sexuality
ディズニーアニメと多様化する社会

國友 万裕　安田 優

松本 恵美　井上 裕子　長岡 亜生　轟 里香　村上 裕美　船本 弘史　須田 久美子

英宝社

音声ファイルのダウンロード方法

英宝社ホームページ（http://www.eihosha.co.jp/）の
「テキスト音声ダウンロード」バナーをクリックすると、
音声ファイルダウンロードページにアクセスできます。

From *Diversity in Disney Films:*
Critical Essays on Race, Ethnicity, Gender and Sexuality

© 2013 Edited by Johnson Cheu by permission of McFarland &
Company, Inc., Box 611, Jefferson NC28640.
www.mcfarlandpub.com
through Japan Uni Agency, Inc. Tokyo

はじめに

　本テキストの編注者 2 人は，2013 年に英宝社から『アビリティとアメリカン・フィルム』という英語テキストを出版しました。このテキストは 2004 年に出された *America on Film* の改訂版（2009）から抜粋したもので，アメリカ映画のなかで，階級・人種・ジェンダー・セクシュアリティ・ディスアビリティがどう描かれているのかを検証していくものです。

　それまで，階級・人種・ジェンダーに関連するテキストはあったものの，セクシュアリティ（同性愛・異性愛・両性愛）の問題を扱うテキストはほとんどなく，その部分では先駆的なテキストだったかと思われます。セクシュアリティの問題はセンシティブなテーマですし，このテキストを使用するにあたって，不安な面もありました。学生たちの中には，実際にセクシュアリティの問題で悩んでいる学生はいるはずで，無神経な発言をしてしまうと，彼らを深く傷つけることが予想され，慎重に授業を進めることになりました。

　しかし，この 5 年の間にセクシュアリティをめぐる状況は大きく変わりました。何よりも 2015 年にアメリカ最高裁が同性婚を認めたことは大きなことでした。日本でも，LGBT（レズビアン，ゲイ，バイセクシャル，トランスジェンダー）という言葉が一般的になり，LGBT を差別する政治家の進退問題が問われるなど，社会は LGBT を理解し，受容する方向へと大きく流れていることが肌で感じられます。LGBT であることはその人たちにとっては必然的であるということ，人間の性は画一的ではないということは，共通認識になってきたように思われます。映画の世界でも，黒人のゲイ男性を主人公にした『ムーン・ライト』（2016），女性同士のラブストーリー『キャロル』（2015），世界で初めて性転換をした男性を描く『リリーのすべて』（2015），男性同士のラブストーリー『君の名前で僕を呼んで』（2017）など，様々な映画が登場し，高い評価を受けています。またたくさんの人物が登場するアンサンブルものでは，その中に必ずゲイの人を登場させて，ポリティカルコレクトネスに配慮されるようにもなりました。

　本テキストはディズニーと多様性とを論じた *Diversity in Disney Films* からの抜粋です。「ディズニー映画で社会を読み解く !?」と聞くと，ディズニー映画は子供向けなのにそんなことができるのか，と考える人もいるかもしれませんが，まだ批判能力のない子供達だからこそ，描かれているステレオタイプと偏見をそのまま内面化してしまいます。これまで，『シンデレラ』『白雪姫』『眠れる森の美女』などは，従順で美しい女性であれば，白馬の王子が救いに来てくれるという伝統的なジェンダーを女の子たちの脳裏に刷り込むものだとフェミニストの

批判を浴びてきましたが，本テキストでは，さらに『ムーラン』『ライオンキング』『ポカホンタス』などにも話を広げ，女性ジェンダーのみならず，男性ジェンダーの問題やトランスジェンダーの問題などの考察もなされています。

　アカデミックな研究書なので，本書がターゲットとするのは，比較的高い英語運用能力を身につけた学生となります。大学入学時，リメディアル教育を必要とする学生群がいる一方，初等・中等教育が理想とする，あるいはそれ以上の英語学習成果を上げた学生群も存在します。後者の割合が全体としては低めになってきたため，上級英語学習者に適した教材も不足気味に思えるようになってきました。本書はその手薄な部分を補完するために開発された教材です。大学英語教育は学生を着実にステップアップさせる必要があります。上級英語学習者を更なる高みへと導くことが求められるのです。ディズニーをモチーフにして，社会を分析する映画論を読み解いていくことで，学習者は読解力だけでなく，高度な言語運用に欠かせない分析力や批判的思考力をも身につけ，考えを深化することができます。加えて，自らの考えを発信するための語彙，表現，議論のレベルを高めるタスクも用意されています。

　このテキストを読むことで，大学生たちが，学術ものの英語を読むことに慣れ，また映画や社会についての新たな見方を習得してくれることを期待しています。

國友万裕・安田優

Contents

Chapter 01 : Progressive Era Protagonists; Cold War and Mentors (1)_____ *6*

Chapter 02 : Progressive Era Protagonists; Cold War and Mentors (2)_____ *11*

Chapter 03 : Honor Through Heterosexuality_____ *16*

　コラム① 　愛されるディズニー_____ *20*

Chapter 04 : Reflecting on the Self_____ *21*

Chapter 05 : Making a Man_____ *25*

Chapter 06 : Performing Meerkat and Warthog_____ *30*

　コラム② 　ジェンダー_____ *35*

Chapter 07 : "Hakuna Matata" : A Problem-Free Philosophy? (1)_____ *36*

Chapter 08 : "Hakuna Matata" : A Problem-Free Philosophy? (2)_____ *41*

Chapter 09 : "Carnivores! Oy!" : Disney and the Jewish Question_____ *46*

　コラム③ 　LGBT_____ *51*

Chapter 10 : Mean Ladies: Transgendered Villains in Disney Films (1)_____ *52*

Chapter 11 : Mean Ladies: Transgendered Villains in Disney Films (2)_____ *57*

Chapter 12 : Mean Ladies: Transgendered Villains in Disney Films (3)_____ *62*

　コラム④ 　多様性を認め合う社会へ_____ *67*

Chapter 13 : Mean Ladies: Transgendered Villains in Disney Films (4)_____ *68*

Chapter 14 : Mean Ladies: Transgendered Villains in Disney Films (5)_____ *73*

Chapter 15 : Mean Ladies: Transgendered Villains in Disney Films (6)_____ *78*

CHAPTER 01

Progressive Era Protagonists; Cold War and Mentors (1)

00 Warm-up

映画『ピノキオ／ *Pinocchio*』（1940），『ダンボ／ *Dumbo*』（1941），『バンビ／ *Bambi*』（1942）の主要な登場人物と物語のあらすじについてリサーチをし，英語で簡潔に紹介しましょう。インターネットやこれらの映画に関する書籍を活用し，PowerPoint なども用いて，オーディエンスのことも考慮しながらわかりやすく発表することを心がけましょう。

01 Vocabulary

次の下線部の表現の意味を例文から推測し，下欄の語群①から訳語を選びましょう。また，その言い換えとして最適な英語表現を下欄の語群②から選びましょう。

例文	語群①	語群②
1. The welcome party was unfortunately the **obverse** of a successful evening.		
2. Numerous studies have **laud**ed the benefits of a high fiber diet over the years.		
3. The tall building over there **exemplifi**es the style of architecture which was popular in the 18th century.		
4. What the soldier did was nothing but a **manifestation** of his love for his country.		
5. The hot sun **enervate**d my wife to the point of collapse.		
6. Those Business groups have tried to **disseminate** the belief that their own profitability means jobs and high wages for everyone.		
7. The teacher said, "If you **marginalize** a minority group, you should be required to take a class specifically about that group."		
8. They were physically confined, worked slavishly, and often treated in a **demeaning** manner.		
9. Directors **underscore**d the critical importance of structural reforms to help boost investor confidence.		
10. He was extremely **dejected** after his wife's death.		

語群①

(a) 広める, (b) 強調する, (c) 〜の良い例となる, (d) 屈辱的な, (e) 現れ・顕現, (f) 落胆した, (g) 称賛する (h) 無視する・軽んじる, (i) 気力を奪う・弱める, (j) 反対の状態

語群②

（ア）causing someone to lose his or her dignity and the respect of others, （イ）to spread something (information, ideas, etc.) to as many people as possible, （ウ）the act of appearing or becoming clear, （エ）to make a person or a group of people unimportant in an unfair way, （オ）unhappy, sad and dispirited, （カ）to make you feel tired and weak, （キ）to emphasize the fact that something is important, （ク）to praise someone or something, （ケ）the opposite of a particular situation or feeling, （コ）to be a very typical example of something

02 Reading

In his study *Babes in Tomorrowland: Walt Disney and the Making of the American Child, 1930-1960*, Nicholas Sammond traces the emergence and development of the Disney canon against the changing backdrop of child-rearing theory and practice that coincides with Disney's rise to prominence, Disney's celebration by child-care experts as positive media, and the company's changing ethos in cold war America. Sammond's charge is to trace how the early-century critique of the movies as potentially denigrating to children's characters makes the **obverse** possible: one can also argue that movies can contribute to children's moral growth. Disney, he demonstrates, built upon this possibility. Once identified as a positive influence, the company consciously cultivates that image.

Sammond's second major focus is related to that cultivation. Sammond argues that Walt Disney himself— his past, his work ethic, and his status as a self-made man—is best understood as a prototype for the ideal "generic child," the goal to which training of children attained in the late 30s and early 40s. Not only are Disney films **laud**ed for their positive influence; Disney's characters are assumed to embody Disney's characteristics. Thus, the theory went, children who see Disney films imbibed the qualities that made Disney who he was.

The 1930s progressive scripts for reforming childcare practices, Sammond argues, stressed conformity, and parental regulation of needs and drives: supported by intense scrutiny of the child, these scripts promised eventual internalization of these privileged values. On the one hand were texts that stress fears of children unsupervised and improperly trained, and on the other were texts that **exemplify** positive outcomes when the child was properly raised. Sammond cautions, however, that norms by which such judgments were measured had been derived from white middle class children. Thus the normal child that cultural texts prized, sought and attempted to form was a white middle class child. (A)As Sammond makes clear, for a 1940s audience primed on child-studies of the '30s, the preoccupation of *Pinocchio*, *Bambi*, and *Dumbo* with regulating and normalizing children would be these films' most significant theme.

For Sammond, *Pinocchio* is the **manifestation** of that "normal" generic child and the social hopes and worries invested in him. Sammond argues that the values that the Blue Fairy charges Pinocchio with demonstrating—goodness, bravery and truth—are values of the white middle class, and the trials are also class-focused. Drawn to the stage, then lying about how he landed in Stromboli's cage, Pinocchio is barely recovered when he falls prey to new temptations. During the trip to Pleasure Island, Pinocchio enjoys drink, tobacco, pool-playing and vandalism in the company of Landwick, a Bowery-accented wastrel who needn't work too hard to seduce Pinocchio away from his unmarked accent and clean habits. The film threatens these boys, transformed into jackasses, with a life of hard labor, convincingly demonstrating Sammond's theory. He argues that Depression-era parents and children learned that "indulgence in the pleasures of the working class ... led to a life as a beast of burden. Ultimately, one was either a manager or managed, and the choices one made determined the outcome."

The same audience that would focus on these points in Pinocchio would likely focus upon Dumbo's quest for a function within the circus economy that will render him, not fame, but simple dignity and acceptance for who he really is, a real identity that is finally revealed when he learns he can fly, and upon the tests that Bambi endures before he can assume his place next to the Great Prince. "Becoming real" for Dumbo and Bambi resonates with gaining autonomous selfhood and Sammond explains that the 1940s audience would code this cultural pinnacle of maturation as "self-management." These films, Sammond indicates, are shaped by 1930s cultural emphasis on the need to develop autonomy and self-management among a population **enervate**d and made hopeless by the Depression. Sammond demonstrates that Disney's films **disseminate**d these values to a widespread cultural audience, acting as, if you will, surrogate training manuals for parents to use to measure the success of their child-rearing.

(B)Sammond's presentation of the issues and discourses through which 1940s viewers would watch Disney films convinces me that those viewers would focus upon the film's representation of the fetishized "normal" child, even though, he allows, the films did not suggest they had to do it alone. For instance, Jiminy Cricket's presence, Sammond posits, suggested to parents that they "needed help, a conscience to whisper to the child ... someone to steer him past the wrong pleasures" and towards "the rewards of hard work, deferred gratification, and self-control." I suggest that figures like Dooley may be more interested in golden age films for the sake of mentor characters than for their discourse on the child—and perhaps that interest in mentors is justified by the Disney Company's production choices and its subsequent marketing practices that increasingly focus upon the mentor characters.

I turn to *Dumbo* first; because it is wholly a Disney creation, without the source texts that inspired Bambi and Pinocchio, its production choices highlight the adaptive choices made in the other two. In particular, the film's flirtation with a potential critique of class and race is contained through association with animal species that re-directs the narrative to its mentoring story. For example, the gossiping, affected tones of the female elephants starkly contrasts Timothy's class-marked American accent, which in turn contrasts the African American accented hipster discourse of the crows. The accents help predict the narrative arc. One might expect that the female elephants would care for the baby elephant. Yet they are focused wholly on external beauty, and disturbingly aligned with a discourse of racial supremacy. They are, in the words of one of the elephants, a "proud race" and Dumbo's ears alone are enough to make him a "disgrace" to that race. Dumbo is marginalized and then exiled from his kind. Having already earned him the moniker "Dumbo," his ears cause him to bungle the "pyramid of pachyderms" and so to injure the others, and drive him to his desperate **demeaning** turn as a clown, from which Timothy, with the eventual help of the crows, rescues him. Thus the characters' alignment with species and their class and race-marked accents **underscore** a story of dysfunction of racial affinity and **underscore** the need for cross-race

8

mentoring.

Timothy Mouse is this film's answer to Jiminy Cricket, with a similar worldly-wise exterior and a tender heart. (C)Tiny in stature, dressed finely in a ringmaster's hat and tailcoat, draped in gold braid, he's as proud of his appearance as Jiminy, and a stark contrast to his mentee in how he is drawn. Timothy walks on two feet, in contrast to Dumbo's four, and his characteristics are human; in contrast, silent Dumbo wears only a hat and acts like an elephant—most notably, Dumbo sways when standing still, and grasps Timothy's tail in his trunk to follow him. Timothy initially seeks revenge upon the female elephants by scaring them on Dumbo's behalf, but otherwise is content to help Dumbo find possible niches in the circus, and to comfort the little elephant when he is **dejected**. Indeed, the film is careful to echo Jumbo's care for Dumbo in a reprise of the bath scene in which Timothy scrubs the clown makeup from Dumbo's face, and dries his tears. Timothy Mouse, anathema to elephants, and feared by Dumbo on first contact, is the figure who truly cares for little Dumbo, helps him to make his way in the world, and helps him discover his hidden talents.

imbibe　吸収する。
Pinocchio　『ピノキオ』1940 年の映画。
Bambi　『バンビ』1942 年の映画。
Dumbo　『ダンボ』1941 年の映画。
Geppetto　ゼペット。ピノキオの生みの親の人形職人。
Jiminy Cricket　ジミニー・クリケット。ゼペット家に入り込んだコオロギ。
The Blue Fairy　ブルー・フェアリー。ピノキオに息を吹き込む金髪の妖精。
Great Prince　バンビの父親。森の王者。
hipster　進んでいる人，流行に敏感な人。
moniker　名前，あだ名。
pachyderm　厚皮動物。

03 *Comprehension Questions*

（A）次の文が本文の内容と一致する場合は T，一致しない場合は F を選びなさい。

① (T・F)	According to Sammond, Disney movies were created based on the possibility that movies could foster children's moral growth.
② (T・F)	It was not difficult for Landwick to seduce Pinocchio to indulge in bad habits.
③ (T・F)	The movies *Bambi* and *Pinocchio* are totally original Disney films, not based on any existing stories
④ (T・F)	Dumbo comes to get his nickname because other elephants thought him to be a shame to their race.
⑤ (T・F)	Dumbo is one of the anthropomorphic Disney characters, who talk a lot like human beings.

（B）本文に関する次の問に答えましょう。

① According to Sammond, what did the 1930s progressive scripts for reforming childcare practices stress?

_____

② What does Sammond think the movies *Dumbo* and *Bambi* are shaped by?

_____

③ What does Timothy Mouse do for *Dumbo* instead of seeking revenge on the female elephants?
_____

04 *Grammatical Structure*

本文中の下線 A，B，C の文の主節における主部と述部を見分けましょう。

	主部	述部
下線 A		
下線 B		
下線 C		

05 *Summary*

次の文中の（　　　）に本文から適語を選んで書き込みましょう。

　　Sammond argued that the 1930s (1.　　　　　) scripts for reforming childcare practices had stressed conformity, and parental (2.　　　　　) of needs and drives. The normal child that cultural texts prized, sought and attempted to form, however, was a white middle class child. For instance, one of the Disney characters Pinocchio is the (3.　　　　　) of the values of the white middle class: goodness, bravery and truth. Through some Disney movies, Depression-era parents and children learned that "indulgence in the pleasures of the working class ... led to a life as a beast of burden…" The films *Dumbo* and *Bambi* can be interpreted in a similar way. "Becoming real" for Dumbo and Bambi resonates with gaining (4.　　　　　) selfhood. As Sammond explained, the 1940s audience coded this cultural pinnacle of maturation as "self-management." These films might have been shaped by the 1930s (5.　　　　　) emphasis on the need to develop autonomy and self-management among a population enervated and made hopeless by the Depression. They also disseminated these values to a widespread cultural audience, acting as (6.　　　　　) training manuals for parents to use to measure the success of their child-rearing. The films can be considered to focus on the importance of the mentor characters. The need for cross-race (7.　　　　　) is emphasized in *Dumbo*.

06 *Discussion/Writing/Presentation*

次の問いかけについて，検討してみましょう。

① In what way are cross-racial understanding and cooperation among individuals of all races important in our society?

② Do you think our thoughts can be affected by movies?

CHAPTER 02
Progressive Era Protagonists; Cold War and Mentors (2)

00 Warm-up

映画『ピノキオ／ *Pinocchio*』（1940）の劇中歌のうち，Gepetto が歌う "Little Wooden Head" と Jiminy Cricket が歌う "When You Wish Upon a Star" についてリサーチをし，歌詞の内容（と可能であれば映画ストーリーとの関連性）について，英語で簡潔に紹介しましょう。PowerPoint に加えて，音声や映像なども活用して発表してみましょう。

01 Vocabulary

次の下線部の表現の意味を例文から推測し，下欄の語群①から訳語を選びましょう。また，その言い換えとして最適な英語表現を下欄の語群②から選びましょう。

例文	語群①	語群②
1. We cannot accept the proposition that equal rights can only be secured by an enforced **commingling** of the two races.		
2. Being a superhero having such great powers and abilities, like being able to read and **manipulate** other people's mind, must be awesome.		
3. We could stay within the **purview** of the law and still made radical changes in our lives.		
4. This course will especially explore the tone combinations that humans consider consonant or **dissonant**.		
5. The brains of young children are **malleable**, and can therefore adapt to what is happening around them.		
6. Art and literature are **immortal** whereas the material achievements of man are just temporary.		
7. The company head **blithely** agreed to the contract without realizing what its consequences would be.		
8. The attack on American democracy is unprecedented in its scale and effect, and has **undermine**d the confidence of Americans in the integrity of the electoral process.		
9. We should not **squash** cockroaches, as they automatically eject an egg-sack if we do that.		
10. Recounting of votes will not be allowed unless there is a **palpable** evidence of an anomaly in counting.		

11

語群①

(a) 不死の・不滅の，(b) 不協和の・意見が合わない，(c) 明白な，(d) 混合，(e) 弱体化させる・覆す，(f) 無頓着に，(g)（権限などの）範囲，(h) 押しつぶす，(i) 操作する，(j) 影響されやすい・従順な

語群②

(ア) lacking harmony, (イ) the limit of someone's responsibility, interest, or activity, (ウ) easily influenced, trained, or controlled, (エ) crush (something) with force so that it becomes out of shape, (オ) to control someone or something in a clever way, (カ) deserving to be remembered forever, (キ) plain to see or comprehend, (ク) in a way that shows a casual indifference considered to be improper, (ケ) lessen the effectiveness, power, or ability of, (コ) mixing; blending

02 Reading

Disney's *Bambi* reveals its focus on mentoring most strongly in its contrast to its source text. Where the film shows an Edenic **commingling** of forest life, Felix Salten's 1928 novel is a dark story of a young deer growing up in a world of deer. Salten's *Bambi* is set in a violent world in which animals fear each other. Bambi's strong shaping influences are his extended family: his aunt's children, some young bucks who eventually become Bambi's rivals, and, occasionally, the Great Prince. Characters like Friend Owl and Thumper are based, if at all, upon the idea of an idea of an animal: Salten barely develops a nameless screech owl and one Mr. Hare who is violently killed by a fox. Thus it seems clearly a Disney innovation when Thumper physically **manipulate**s Bambi's form and shares words of wisdom about kindness and proper vegetable consumption.

Disney's *Pinocchio* is created without a mother at all, of course—the child of Gepetto's carving and painting skill—in a home where all generativity is man's **purview**. The film lingers on Gepetto's creations—clockworks constructed on a cricket's scale, with tiny humanized dramas played out on the hour or at the turn of a key. In a sequence that moves from the natural world to violence, we see first clockwork ducks and birds, and soon a hunter shooting a bird, a drunkard lolling out a window, and finally a mother spanking her child. (A)Shown following Gepetto's song "Little Wooden Head," this small survey of the darker human impulses seems a fitting counterpoint to the disturbing between-ness of the manipulated puppet, who alternately strokes and kicks Figaro; seen through the side of Cleo's bowl, the puppet is revealed in its **dissonant** and distorted essence. Later, when Gepetto is awakened by Pinocchio, now alive but not yet human, falling from the work table, these clockworks are re-animated by Gepetto's gunshot, but soon replaced by clockworks selected by Gepetto and Pinocchio with more positive scenarios—an angelic herald, a mother bird feeding her young, a stately couple dancing. There is something wrong with these creations, Pinocchio among them—a shallowness, a manipulability that is highlighted by

a reprise of Gepetto's puppetry when he controls the now-living Pinocchio by manipulating his suspenders—but of course that is the story's point: even the least **malleable** of creations can be manipulated by others unless they develop bravery, truthfulness and unselfishness sufficient to become "real."

Pinocchio seems allegorical, of course, when his lederhosen and Bavarian hat, and Gepetto's German accent are considered, of the dawning totalitarian commitment of both the Germany his clothes echo, and the Italy from whence his name comes. Those countries, to the American press, seemed to be little more than marionettes being operated at their leaders' wills. Where, the press asked later, when faced with the Nuremberg defense, were their consciences? Perhaps, like Pinocchio's, they could fit inside the brain of a cricket.

Disney's innovations in *Pinocchio* are most revealing of the ethos that may power the Cold War rereading of Disney's Golden Age. For instance, in Collodi's tale, Gepetto wants a child because his wife died, but she is never mentioned in Disney. But Collodi's cricket is changed even more dramatically. Originally, Disney had envisioned a film without the cricket, but early in production, the staff worried that Pinocchio seemed cold and heartless. The cricket was added to house Pinocchio's other half—the conscience that he would eventually internalize. Early story meetings dealt with the difficulty of drawing Jiminy—apparently crickets are pretty frightening in extreme close-up. Yet the commitment to retaining the character was firm. As sketching and scripting moved forward, Disney reputedly predicted "If only I could find someone who could see Jiminy the way he should be. If we can just get him right, he'll become as **immortal** as Mickey Mouse." Indeed. The film might better be called Jiminy Cricket when its final structure is considered.

(B)If Pinocchio is still a wooden head—a tabula rasa—a complete vacuum, but with powers of locomotion and with the ability to choose but no moral or experiential register against which to measure his choices, we could be relieved to know that a conscience has been provided to him. Yet, we should, as viewers, be deeply worried about Pinocchio's lack of preparation for his world, as should Gepetto when he **blithely** sends the puppet-boy to school. Jiminy Cricket's value as Pinocchio's conscience is preemptively **undermine**d as he agrees to be a conscience because of attraction to the Blue Fairy. Preening over his own transformed appearance from vagabond to "Sir Jiminy Cricket," Jiminy unsurprisingly "almost forgot about" "ol' Pinocch." Indeed, his instructions to "give a little whistle" when Pinocchio needs help are about the height of his effectiveness as conscience. Drawn as a womanizer and a scamming opportunist, for all the good he does Pinocchio one could almost wish for a reprise of Collodi's choice in the original tale: there, the Cricket gets **squash**ed.

Yet, the film is given to Jiminy as the focalizing character. Through him we witness the story. The film opens on him, and purports to recount how he learned the lesson that, "When You Wish Upon a Star," a person's—or cricket's—dreams may be realized. In the opening sequence, the camera even replicates his perspective, mimicking his hopping toward Gepetto's house, and it closes on his thanks to the Blue Fairy and shows him rewarded with his badge. Structurally, we are privy to Gepetto and Pinocchio's story only because Jiminy enters Gepetto's home. While whole scenes do happen outside his vision, the film is consistent enough to be read as being told through his eyes. What's more, Jiminy's character is clearly an American type within an easily traced tradition of the tough-guy with a tender heart. He is streetsmart, wisecracking, an improviser, world-wise yet quick to sympathize with the innocent and weak and just as quick to defend them. His American-ness is underscored in the context of those characters that tempt and exploit Pinocchio. Stromboli, Honest John and the Coachman, in practice and accent, are bastions of the old country and **palpable** threats to Pinocchio, and Jiminy is his only protection.

(C)Just as the film insists on Jiminy's centrality to the story, the importance of Jiminy to Disney as a corporation is also clear. His song, "When You Wish Upon a Star" is more endemic than "It's a Small World": "When You Wish Upon a Star" is played under the company logo at the start and finish of every Disney film, and sampled in most commercials for Disney products and theme parks even today. What's more, in the 1950s Jiminy Cricket appeared regularly on the *Mickey Mouse Club* as the narrator of two segments that purported to teach children about their bodies and good behavior. For Disney, as for American audiences in the late 1950s, the significant character in these coming of age classics is not the innocent and naïve child, but the American mentor who guides him.

These three films, in their original moment, certainly lent themselves to a reading that meditates on the meaning of childhood in 1940s America, and on social concerns with producing children who are "brave, good and true." Read against the backdrop of 1955-60, incipient meanings in the old scripts surface and the role of singular Americans reaching across race difference, recoded as species boundaries, to help weaker "species" seems more emphatic. Neither reading may be definitively attributed to Walt Disney productions as a final or fixed meaning; rather, perhaps, what surfaces in a reading of a text changes to serve its cultural moment.

Friend Owl 森のフクロウ。森の長。
Thumper とんすけ。バンビと最初に親しくなるウサギ。
Figaro フィガロ。ゼペットの飼っている猫。
Cleo クレオ。ゼペットの飼っている金魚。
lederhosen レーダーホーセン。ドイツからオーストラリアで，男性によって着用される肩紐付きの皮の半ズボン。
Bavarian hat チロリアン・ハット。

03 *Comprehension Questions*

（A）次の文が本文の内容と一致する場合は T，一致しない場合は F を選びなさい。

① (T・F)	The film version of *Bambi* has a much gloomier story, where animals torment one another, than its source text.
② (T・F)	The U.S. press considered Germany and Italy to be just like puppets being controlled by dictatorial puppeteers.
③ (T・F)	*Jiminy Cricket* could be a more suitable title, considering the structure of the movie *Pinocchio*.
④ (T・F)	The audience of *Pinocchio* is to experience the story through the character Gepetto.
⑤ (T・F)	It is Jiminy Cricket who sings "When You Wish Upon a Star," which is played exclusively at the beginning of every Disney film.

（B）本文に関する次の問に答えましょう。

① How does Felix Salten describe the characters of a screech owl and a rabbit in his novel *Bambi*?

_____

② When can we consider the character Pinocchio to be allegorical of Germany's and Italy's commitment to the rising totalitarianism?

_____

③ How is Jiminy Cricket's Americanness highlighted in the film?

_____

04 *Grammatical Structure*

本文中の下線 A，B，C の文の主節における主部と述部を見分けましょう。

	主部	述部
下線 A		
下線 B		
下線 C		

05 *Summary*

次の文中の（　　　）に本文から適語を選んで書き込みましょう。

　The Disney film *Pinocchio* can be interpreted from the socio-cultural viewpoint. The way the protagonist Pinocchio is treated there suggests the idea that even the least (1.　　　　) of creations can be (2.　　　　) by others unless they develop bravery, truthfulness and unselfishness sufficient to become "real." To some extent, Pinocchio also seems (3.　　　　) of the dawning totalitarian (4.　　　　) of both Germany and Italy. Another important character is Jiminy Cricket, who is supposed to be the (5.　　　　) that Pinocchio eventually internalizes. Through his eyes, the audience is supposed to (6.　　　　) what is going on in the film. In a way, Jiminy is obviously an American type within an easily traced tradition of the tough-guy with a tender heart. In the 1950s, this character was thought to have functioned as the American (7.　　　　) who guided innocent and naïve children.

06 *Discussion/Writing/Presentation*

次の問いかけについて，検討してみましょう。

① Do you think using anthropomorphic/personified animal characters is an effective way of conveying social or cultural messages to the audience? Why or why not?

② The same story can be interpreted in numerous ways. What do you think makes it possible to do that?

CHAPTER 03

Honor Through Heterosexuality

00 *Warm-up*

映画『ムーラン／ *Mulan*』（1998）の主要な登場人物と物語のあらすじ（時代背景を含む）についてリサーチをし，英語で簡潔に紹介しましょう。PowerPoint なども用いて，わかりやすく発表することを心がけましょう。

01 *Vocabulary*

次の下線部の表現の意味を例文から推測し，下欄の語群①から訳語を選びましょう。また，その言い換えとして最適な英語表現を下欄の語群②から選びましょう。

例文	語群①	語群②
1. Their **ostensible** goal was to clean up political corruption, but their real aim was quite different.		
2. If you are going into teaching, generosity, for example, is a necessary **commodity**.		
3. The village **matchmaker** succeeded in arranging more than 100 highly satisfactory marriages.		
4. Mulan was considered to be a beautiful and **demure** woman in her village		
5. Mahatma Gandhi **reiterate**d his intentions to leave for England.		
6. The private key is supposed to be known only to the **proprietor** of the building.		
7. Most members of the significant Protestant minority **adhere**d to the Calvinist faith.		
8. The principal **rite** of many Native Americans is the peyote ceremony.		
9. All the teachers of the school are expected to **fall in line** with the new regulations.		
10. The ceremony **culminate**d in a great round dance where everybody united in a great circle.		

語群①

(a) 取り澄ました・おとなしい，(b) 忠実である，(c) 〜と同調する，(d) 仲人，(e) 何度も繰り返す，(f) 儀式，(g) 見せかけの，(h) 保持者・所有者，(i) 最高点に達する，(j) 利点・役に立つもの

語群②

(ア) someone who arranges marriages for others, (イ) to stay, state, or perform again or several times, (ウ) a traditional ceremony, especially a religious one, (エ) appearing to be true, or stated by someone to be true, but possibly false, (オ) reserved, modest, and shy, (カ) the owner of a business, or a holder of property, (キ) reach the highest point, (ク) something that is useful or necessary, (ケ) to be a devoted follower or supporter, (コ) to obey or agree to

02 Reading

Two of the **ostensible** themes of the film are established through the first song, "Honor to Us All": in particular, that honor is the most precious **commodity** an individual can provide the community; and that fulfilling societal imperatives, fitting in to one's (gender) role, is difficult but necessary for survival. In order to gain the former one must succeed in the latter. (A) As Mulan prepares to meet the **matchmaker**, who holds the girls' place in society in the balance, she copies notes onto her arm as if about to take a test she's ill-equipped to pass. (B)The necessities for impressing the matchmaker do not reside within Mulan but must be placed on her as visible indicators: "quiet, demure, graceful, polite, delicate, refined, poised, punctual." These characteristics are not innate and do not come from within Mulan; rather, they are to be learned and **reiterate**d, to be placed on the body, just as make-up and fancy dress, in order to designate her as female.

Both visually and lyrically the scene demonstrates that Mulan (and, by extension, all other girls), must submit to a feminizing process. Mulan, before the intervention of society's restrictive gender requirements, is not made of the right materials to be formed into a proper woman, which in this context is equivalent to a proper bride. She is substandard in the eyes of the women who mark—and make—girls who bring honor to their families. Nevertheless, because every girl must become a bride (read: truly female), Mulan undergoes the transformative process through which she will be created. As her mother and grandmother take Mulan from shop to shop, we learn exactly what is required to be a girl and thus bring "honor to us all." (C)Each **proprietor** of femininity lists the extensive qualities that make a bride, and each lesson for becoming female is both oral and visual: Mulan is told what she must be and then made into that model. Rather than adhering to the demands of her family role, Mulan continually resists her transformation. She is pushed and pulled by hairdressers and costumers, always looking pained and uncomfortable in her own body. Every characteristic, even a tiny waist, is fabricated rather than natural, and none are essentially linked to the biological "fact" of Mulan's sex. Like the make-up painted on her face, the above qualities are culturally constructed markers of femininity that one assumes as a **rite** of passage into womanhood.

But one cannot pass through this rite without finally meeting the local matchmaker and earning her approval. She will determine a girl's future position in relation to society, and the girls recognize the consequences when they equate her with an undertaker. The power this woman yields, more frightening

木蘭と父の像（新郷市）Kruuth

than death itself, emphasizes the necessity of heterosexual approbation in order to secure a place in society. Mulan stumbles through the marketplace, trying to catch up and—literally and figuratively—**fall in line** with the other potential brides. While they smile and repeat the hope of bringing honor, each girl looking nearly identical, Mulan stares ahead in disbelief that she must be like them in appearance and action. Their transformation **culminate**s through finding husbands and integrating them fully into the heterosexual matrix by which they will be recognized as women. Thus a woman is delineated by her appearance only in that it leads to heterosexuality. The song and scenes make clear that a daughter can only bring honor to herself and her family by becoming a bride. Without fulfilling her assigned gender role through marriage she and her family merit no honor, nor can she honor the Emperor by bearing sons. In this world Mulan has no other options than wife and mother, they "are presented as the ultimate goal" for all girls, "suggesting that there are no 'female' alternatives in relationships."

Mulan 1998 年の映画。古代中国を舞台にし，中国の伝説『花木蘭』をモデルにしている。
poised 落ち着いた。

03 *Comprehension Questions*

（A）次の文が本文の内容と一致する場合は T，一致しない場合は F を選びなさい。

① （T・F）	In this film, honor is the most important factor for each family.
② （T・F）	Mulan was willing to fit in to her role as a daughter for her family.
③ （T・F）	Matchmakers had as much power over girls and their families as an executioner.
④ （T・F）	The song "Honor to Us All" gives shape to the image of the ideal woman at that time.
⑤ （T・F）	The ultimate goal for girls was to be a wife and mother through marriage.

（B）本文に関する次の問に答えましょう。

① Describe "the two of the ostensible themes" of the film.

_____

② Explain about "a rite of passage into womanhood" in the passage.

_____

③ How was each girl educated to pass through a feminizing process?

_____

04 Grammatical Structure

本文中の下線 A，B，C の文の主節における主部と述部を見分けましょう。

	主部	述部
下線 A		
下線 B		
下線 C		

05 Summary

次の文中の（　　　）に本文から適語を選んで書き込みましょう。

　The film *Mulan* impresses on us that Mulan helps her family with her brave decision and contributions. But through the passage, it is shown that *Mulan* is given another important role to bring honor as a daughter of her family: to be chosen as a bride by a local (1.　　　　). The ideal women can be seen in the first song, " (2.　　　　) to Us All" In the song, it is clear that a daughter can only bring honor to herself and her family by becoming a (3.　　　　) *Mulan* is (4.　　　　) from this goal, however, she tries herself to adjust social (5.　　　　) role. Although Mulan resists her (6.　　　　) as a rite of passage into womanhood, she accepts her role in her family. *Mulan* has no other (7.　　　　) than wife and mother, presented as the ultimate goal for girls.

06 Discussion/Writing/Presentation

次の問いかけについて，検討してみましょう。

① Have you ever been forced to be like a lady? What did you feel reluctant to do?

② Some people claim that married couples should have separate family names. Do you agree or disagree?

コラム①愛されるディズニー

　アメリカン・フィルム・インスティテュート（AFI）がアメリカ映画100年シリーズの一環として，2008年にアニメ映画のベストテンを発表しました。結果は以下の通りです。

1　　『白雪姫 』（*Snow White And The Seven Dwarfs* 1937）
2　　『ピノキオ』（*Pinocchio* 1940）
3　　『バンビ』（*Bambi* 1942）
4　　『ライオン・キング』（*The Lion King* 1994）
5　　『ファンタジア』（*Fantasia* 1940）
6　　『トイ・ストーリー』（*Toy Story* 1995）
7　　『美女と野獣』（*Beauty And The Beast* 1991）
8　　『シュレック』（*Shrek* 2001）
9　　『シンデレラ』（*Cinderella* 1950）
10　　『ファインディング・ニモ』（*Finding Nemo* 2003）

　8位の『シュレック』はドリームワークス作品であり，ディズニーとは無関係ですが，ほかは全てディズニー映画（『トイ・ストーリー』『ファインディング・ニモ』を制作したピクサー・アニメーション・スタジオはディズニーの子会社）であり，圧倒的なディズニーの強さを見せつけます。

　上位の『白雪姫』『ピノキオ』『バンビ』『ファンタジア』は，第二次世界大戦の頃の映画ですし，80年もの月日が流れているわけですが，今見ても錆びていません。絵を見ているだけでも楽しいですし，話の展開はわかっていても，巧妙な語り口に引き込まれます。とりわけ，『白雪姫』はアメリカ映画ベスト100（2007年発表）でも34位に食い込んでおり，不動の名作と言っていいでしょう。

　さらにディズニーは実写映画も製作しており，『メリー・ポピンズ』（1964）はアニメと実写の合成映画で，主演のジュリー・アンドリュースにアカデミー賞をもたらした名作です。この映画の製作の経緯を描いた『ウォルト・ディズニーの約束』（2014）ではトム・ハンクスがウォルト・ディズニー役を演じています。さらに，2018年には『メリー・ポピンズ　リターン』がエミリー・ブラントの主演で公開されました。

　加えて，ディズニーと言えば，リゾートパークでも有名。筆者の教えている学生のなかには，京都から夜行バスで東京ディズニーランドに行って，1日遊んで，そのまま夜行バスで京都へ帰り，翌朝には大学の授業に出ている学生もいます。若いから体力があるからこそできることなのですが，疲れを吹き飛ばすような魅力がディズニーにはあるのでしょう。

　万人に愛されるディズニーですが，そこには秘密のメッセージが込められています。このテキストを勉強しながら，たまには批判的な視点からディズニーを考えてみましょう。

CHAPTER
04

Reflecting on the Self

00 Warm-up

映画『ムーラン / *Mulan*』(1998) の主人公は，社会や文化が規定する性役割に沿わない異性装を行いますが，女らしい服装あるいは男らしい服装とはどのようなものでしょうか。古今東西において，女性と男性それぞれに対して，どのような服装が割り当てられてきたのか，またそれらの服装にはどのような意味が付与されてきたのかについてリサーチをし，簡潔に発表してみましょう。

01 Vocabulary

次の下線部の表現の意味を例文から推測し，下欄の語群①から訳語を選びましょう。また，その言い換えとして最適な英語表現を下欄の語群②から選びましょう。

例文	語群①	語群②
1. The famous scholar **conflate**d several different versions of the text into one.		
2. Stay-at-home mothers are no longer the **norm** in today's society.		
3. The woman was too drunk to attempt to **dissimulate** her loneliness.		
4. The man does not understand that the elegance of his girlfriend is just a **facade**.		
5. **Cross-dressing** is grounded in a highly logical and universal desire, and it is also a form of self-expression.		
6. There are few legal **constraint**s on the sale of firearms in the United States.		
7. The girl cut her hair short, wore **armor** and fought with a sword in battle.		
8. Henry arrived at the house in **disguise** as an old French artist named Pierre.		
9. Archaeological evidence **attest**s to the presence of stone-tool-using people in the area as long as 5,000 years ago.		
10. Kevin did not **admonish** his sons and daughters who were drinking too much late at night in the bar.		

語群①

(a) 偽り隠す， (b) 制約・強制・束縛， (c) 諭す・戒める・忠告する， (d) 標準・基準・規範，
(e) 甲冑， (f) 証明する， (g) 合成する・まとめる， (h) 男装 / 女装，(i) 見せかけ， (j) 変装

21

語群②

(ア) a way of altering one's appearance to conceal one's identity, (イ) to wear the clothes of the opposite sex (ウ) behavior that is very controlled and not natural, (エ) to combine two or more things, (オ) to give proof or be evidence that something is true, (カ) a false appearance or way of behaving that hides what someone or something is really like, (キ) to hide your real thoughts, feelings, or intentions, (ク) metal clothing that soldiers wore in the Middle Ages to protect their bodies, (ケ) to advise someone to do something earnestly, (コ) something that is usual or expected

02 Reading

After the matchmaker declares, "You may look like a bride, but you will never bring your family honor!" Mulan returns home, and, upon seeing her father's hopeful face, turns away to reflect (literally) on her position. (A)In Mulan's mind (and within society), the terms "bride" and "daughter" are **conflate**d, and following the matchmaker's chastisement, Mulan questions exactly what part she is meant to play. The film takes the notion of the perfomativity of gender a step further and creates a literal metaphor for Mulan's identity questions in the form of theatrical roles. As Judith Butler indicates, "Perfomativity is thus not a singular 'act,' for it is always a reiteration of a **norm** or set of norms, and to the extent that it acquires an act-like status in the present, it conceals or **dissimulate**s the conventions of which it is a repetition ... its apparent theatricality is produced to the extent that its historicity remains dissimulated." The preparations for meeting the matchmaker reduce the performativity—the repetition and citation of gender norms—to a set of acts that one exhibits in the moment, as if that perfomativity were a conscious choice; thus the dressing and making-up process conceals the historical actuality of required and unconscious reiteration of gender norms.

Indeed, to the extent that one declares "It's a girl!" at birth, the naming of the girl "initiates the process by which a certain 'girling' is compelled, the term ... governs the formation of a corporeally enacted femininity that never fully approximates the norm.... Femininity is thus not the product of a choice, but the forcible citation of a norm." Once Mulan realizes that she cannot approximate or properly cite the feminine norm, she questions only herself and her "performance" rather than the norm itself. Yet, as Garber notes, "Gender roles and categories are most vulnerable to critique when they are most valorized, when their rules, codes, and expectations are most ardently coveted and admired." Though Disney impugns the extravagant means through which a girl conforms to gender expectations, it never challenges the expectation itself. Rather than critiquing the institution that requires a proper wife to be only silent and beautiful, the film instead focuses on the crisis an individual experiences when she does not meet the requirement. The paternal edict "I know my place, it is time you learned yours" commands Mulan to assimilate a preconceived gender role rather than rebel and form a new one.

Asking who she sees in her reflection underscores the importance of the physical manifestations of one's gender role in Mulan's world. When she looks at herself Mulan shows only sadness at what appears before her. (B)The reflection of what should be the perfect bride and daughter does not touch the reality of what is underneath the female **facade**. Both of Mulan's reflections—the painted and unpainted faces—are conveyed on the temple stones of her family shrine. Placed there to honor the Fa family ancestors, the stones represent both the duty Mulan owes her father and her inability to fulfill that duty in her current form. She realizes that "only by changing her outer appearance can [she] reflect her inner identity." That Mulan does not recognize the girl in her reflection, that she reflects her inner identity via **cross-dressing**, raises the question of whom (and what gender) Mulan wishes to enact. Although "[t]hematically this song functions as a monologue through which the heroine expresses her longing for an accredited individuality," that accredited individuality is inextricable from a condoned gender role. Disney reinforces the cultural **constraint** that one's identity is dependent on the successful realization of one's gender imperatives through Mulan's personal crisis after she fails to earn the matchmaker's approbation.

Mulan sees her identity as wrapped up in the artifice of sartorial markers so that, when she does not receive the designation of woman in her female clothes and make-up, she begins to doubt what kind of identity she is to have/perform. She seems unaware of the implications of this mode of gender construction, yet when Mulan passes as male by employing the right clothes, she demonstrates that both her feminine clothes and her **armor** are costumes that do not actually correspond to the gender of the person whom they cover. Thus, as Garber notes, "Transvestism, deployed strategically as **disguise**, uncovers as it covers, reveals the masquerade that is already in place." Mulan may be biologically identified as female, but, as the matchmaker scene and the ensuing song "Reflection" **attest**, she does not fulfill the gender roles required of her. (C)Trying to be the "perfect" bride or the "perfect" daughter is a masquerade already in place and literalized via the white face paint she wears at the bride selection. When she decides to run away, trying to "learn her place" as her father **admonish**ed, Mulan trades one mask for another, and the success she experiences with the male disguise only emphasizes her previous failure with the female one.

chastisement 懲戒。
Judith Butler (1956~) ジュディス・バトラー，アメリカの哲学者。著書『ジェンダー・トラブル』(1990) はフェミニズムやクィア理論に大きな影響を与えた。
approximate 近くする。
valorize 安定させる。
impugn 非難する。
edict 勅令。

03 Comprehension Questions

（A）次の文が本文の内容と一致する場合は T，一致しない場合は F を選びなさい。

① (T・F)	The matchmaker accepted Mulan as a bride who can bring honor to her family.
② (T・F)	The preparation for meeting the matchmaker encourages girls to develop their performativity.
③ (T・F)	Femininity means that girls act by their conscious choices in the course of preparation for meeting the matchmaker.
④ (T・F)	Disney tries to introduce silent and beautiful wives as the model of ideal women.
⑤ (T・F)	When *Mulan* wears female clothes and make-up, she can feel identified with other women.

（B）本文に関する次の問に答えましょう。

① What does "perfomativity" mean in this passage?

_____

② What does "femininity" mean in this passage?

_____

③ Explain the psychological meaning of "the temple stones of Ma's family shrine".

_____

04 Grammatical Structure

本文中の下線 A，B，C の文の主節における主部と述部を見分けましょう。

	主部	述部
下線 A		
下線 B		
下線 C		

05 Summary

次の文中の（　　　）に本文から適語を選んで書き込みましょう。（同じ番号には同じ語が入ります）

　　The matchmaker declared that Mulan is not a daughter who can bring honor to her family. It means that Mulan cannot take the form of theatrical roles in her society. (1.　　　　　) is another word for a theatrical role. The preparations for meeting the matchmaker decrease (1). Mulan realizes that she cannot act as the (2.　　　) norm to be a bride. It is said that Disney blames this social system, in which a girl tries to fulfill her gender (3.　　　　) for her family. The film focuses on the crisis when Mulan does not meet the (4.　　　　) of her family and society. It is Mulan's personal crisis after she fails the matchmaker's (5.　　　　). Ironically Mulan realizes her inner identity through (6.　　　　). Mulan is biologically identified as a female, but she is accepted by (7.　　　) in her society.

06 Discussion/Writing/Presentation

次の問いかけについて，検討してみましょう。

① Do you think women should do housework more than men should do, while men should support their family by working harder?

② Find a person who is trying to change his/her gender identity. Do some research on that person and present it in class.

CHAPTER 05

Making a Man

00 *Warm-up*

女らしさと男らしさという点に留意しながら，映画『ムーラン / *Mulan*』(1998) の劇中歌である "Honor to Us All" と "I'll Make a Man Out of You" のそれぞれの歌詞（の類似点）について比較・検討し，できる限り平易な英語で発表してみましょう。

01 *Vocabulary*

次の下線部の表現の意味を例文から推測し，下欄の語群①から訳語を選びましょう。また，その言い換えとして最適な英語表現を下欄の語群②から選びましょう。

例文	語群①	語群②
1. In the exhibition near the beach, abstract paintings are **juxtapose**d with beautiful photographs.		
2. His skating **prowess** was demonstrated in the countless skating trophies he won.		
3. The city boasts a **plethora** of marvelous art galleries.		
4. He enjoys reading books full of rhyming sentences with vivid metaphors, **simile**s and puns.		
5. His mother knew, at the deep level of her **psyche**, that her son was innocent.		
6. She **refute**d his argument with numerous facts.		
7. He made a sharp **rejoinder** to her comment on the issue.		
8. A Japanese man died trying to **scale** the Matterhorn.		
9. My brother was sent to **retrieve** the surfboard from the beach.		
10. An injury was **hinder**ing her from playing her best at the international competition.		

語群①

(a) 精神，(b) すぐれた能力，(c) ～を登る，(d)（対照比較のため）～を並置する，(e) ～の邪魔する，(f) 直喩，(g) ～を（人・場所から）取り戻す，(h) ～を論破 [反論] する，(i) 過多，(j)（乱暴な）返答、言い返し

25

語群②

（ ア ）an amount that is greater than is needed or can be used, （ イ ）the mind; your deepest feelings and attitudes, （ ウ ）to make it difficult for somebody to do something or something to happen, （ エ ）to climb to the top of something very high and steep, （ オ ）to prove that something is wrong, （ カ ）a word or phrase that compares something to something else, using the words like or as, （ キ ）great skill at doing something, （ ク ）to bring or get something back, especially from a place where it should not be, （ ケ ）a reply, especially a quick, critical or amusing one, （ コ ）to put people or things together, especially in order to show a contrast or a new relationship between them

02 Reading

If "Honor to Us All" functions as an account of the constructedness of female gender, then its counterpart "I'll Make a Man Out of You," which plays over the montage of the soldier's training, both **juxtapose**s and makes explicit the contention that gender is a cultural product. Mulan's transformative toilette is a "subconscious recognition that 'woman' in patriarchal society is conceived of as an artifact, and that the logical next step is the recognition that 'man' is likewise not fact but artifact, himself constructed." The film exploits this recognition in both senses via the subsequent scenes at the training camp. Rather than copying crib notes onto her arm to pass as a proper daughter and bride, Mulan—now dressed in male clothing and named Ping—carries Mushu, a small dragon guardian, through the camp, listening to his whispered guidance on how to "act like a man." Thus the Wu Shu camp functions on two levels: training new recruits to be soldiers as well as training Mulan to be a man. If "wife" is the cultural artifact of woman in the film, then "soldier" is the cultural artifact of man. It is much more common to speak of "making a man" out of some (male) candidate; some martial or sexual exercise will "'make a man' of the hapless boy.... To 'make' a man is to test him." Becoming a man is an active process, requiring some physical or sexual **prowess** on the part of the subject. Becoming a woman, in contrast, is a passive process, to be enacted upon a silent object. Though Shang takes the rhetorically active place within the song (he is the one "making" a man of others), Ping and the other soldiers equally participate in the process of their making; they learn hand-to-hand combat, archery, rocket launching, and a **plethora** of physical activities to become their own agents of achieving manhood.

However, qualifiers of manhood are not as distinct as those for womanhood. Whereas the women in town tell Mulan exactly how she must look to be female, descriptions of being a man are cloaked in **simile**. The comparisons to elements of nature attempt to frame manliness as part of the natural world and thus not constructed by conventional society. The use of similes also functions to obscure the delineation of exactly *what does* make a "man"; perhaps what lies behind this lyrical vagueness is, according to Garber, a "sneaking feeling that it should not be so easy to 'construct' a 'man.'" For in these lines there are no step-by-step directions for the process of becoming, only the repeated, baritone-voices of the chorus commanding each soldier to "Be a man." The montage sequencing of these scenes provides only evidence of the change the soldiers make into men, not *how* such a change came about—what the characters did to become men. In "Honor to Us All," Mulan receives instructions accompanied by their actions: the woman painting Mulan's face sings about being pale at the same moment she applies the white paint. In contrast to Captain Li's dictates to be a man, the process of becoming a woman is given as an instruction manual and made accessible to any who wishes to learn and mimic it.

Also juxtaposed to the feminine transformation, the male experience is one of physicality and awareness of the body. Mulan is taught that the female body is not for her own use, that its value is only measurable by its attractiveness to future husbands. (A)Her male facade Ping, on the other hand, shows that the masculine body is essential to male self-definition, that it must be fully integrated with the **psyche** to establish gender. Recall that Mushu's first lesson to Mulan in passing is imitating a "man walk" into the training camp. Mushu can tell her what to do to walk like a man, but without knowledge of her capabilities Mulan cannot pass in the eyes of other men. Her near failure to become a man results from her body's inability to attain physical goals despite her emotional and intellectual desire to do so.

(B)Though the film attempts to place male and female genders on opposing sides of an intractable boundary, by relying on a binary structure to support its definition of these genders it in fact exposes a contradiction. As Eve Sedgwick observes in her analysis of binaries, valorized terms are nonetheless dependent upon subordinate terms for meaning. The film emphasizes that women are not considered equal to men—indeed, even after Mulan defeats Shan-Yu, the emperor's counselor **refute**s the claim that "she's a hero" with the **rejoinder** "she's a woman." Furthermore, as Shang and the other soldiers reveal, manhood is not only an active process of making a man but also defined in opposition to woman/girlhood ("Be a man.... Don't be such a girl"). Thus manhood is not an entity unto itself, separate from womanhood; rather, it depends on the latter for its constitution.

As in the confrontation with the matchmaker, Mulan nearly fails to become a fully realized participant in the heterosexual matrix. Neither man nor woman, she would be unmarked, non-existent within her community and within discourse. Shang tells Ping to go home asking, disbelieving that he can make a man out of the novice. Mulan disobeys the command and works on her own to prove her manhood. She must **scale** the high wooden pole, phallic in its near impossibility of being conquered, with weights that represent strength and discipline to **retrieve** an arrow at the top. (C)Though Ping has gone through military training and followed Shang's orders, helped (and more often **hinder**ed) by Mushu, she has not attempted anything alone. Now, with her family's honor and her own existence being threatened, Mulan must rely only on herself to become a man. She must transition from passive object upon which gender is written and become the subject-agent that claims a gender and a role in the community. Thus in answer to Shang's question of how he could make a man out of Ping, Mulan demonstrates that *he* cannot; as the cross-dressed figure it is up to Mulan to make herself a man, to move from passive object to active subject. The most important step here is the claiming of her bodily power and integrating physical and mental strength to "make it" to the top, to "make herself a man." Because she is able to scale the pole when the other men cannot, it appears that her "power inheres in her blurred gender, in the fact of her cross-dressing, and not—despite the stereotypical romantic ending—in *either* of her gendered identities."

montage モンタージュ　映画用語。複数のカットをつなぎ合わせて，意味を生み出していく技法。フォトモンタージュと混同しないように注意。

Eve Sedgwick イブ・セジウィック (1950~2009)　アメリカの文学研究者，ジェンダー理論家。彼女が『男同士の絆』（名古屋大学出版協会）で提唱したホモソーシャルの理論は 21 世紀初頭，アカデミズムの世界に大きな影響を与えた。

manhood　男性性・男らしさを指す語。20 世紀までは内面的な「男らしさ」という意味でこの語が使われていた。しかし，21 世紀になると男らしさの捉え方が振る舞いや外見などを指すようになったため，masculinity を使うケースが増えて

いった。
novice 新米。

03 Comprehension Questions

（A）次の文が本文の内容と一致する場合は T，一致しない場合は F を選びなさい。

①	（T・F）	The process of becoming a man is considered passive.
②	（T・F）	In the film Mulan was told precisely how she must appear to be a woman by the women in town.
③	（T・F）	Mulan is taught that the value of the female body is measured by its attractiveness to husbands-to-be.
④	（T・F）	The film stresses that women are regarded as equal to men.
⑤	（T・F）	Mulan goes against Shang's order and works by herself to prove her manhood.

（B）本文に関する次の問に答えましょう。

① What functions does the Wu Shu camp have in the film?

_____

② What was the cause of Mulan's near failure to become a man?

_____

③ What did Shang and the other soldiers reveal in the film?

_____

04 Grammatical Structure

本文中の下線 A，B，C の文の主節における主部と述部を見分けましょう。

	主部	述部
下線 A		
下線 B		
下線 C		

05 Summary

次の文中の（　　　）に本文から適語を選んで書き込みましょう。

　Mulan's transformative toilette is a "subconscious recognition that 'woman' in patriarchal society is conceived of as an artifact, and that the logical next step is the (1.　　　　) that 'man' is likewise not fact but artifact, himself constructed." Becoming a man is an active process, requiring some physical or sexual prowess on the part of the subject. Becoming a woman, in contrast, is a passive process, to be enacted upon a silent object. Juxtaposed to the feminine (2.　　　　), the male experience is one of physicality and (3.   ) of the body. The film emphasizes that women are not considered equal to men. Furthermore, manhood is not only an active process of making a man but also defined in (4.   ) to woman/girlhood. Mulan nearly fails to become a fully realized participant in the (5.   ) matrix. Neither man nor woman, she would be (6.   ), non-existent within her community and within discourse. As the cross-dressed figure it is up to Mulan to make herself a man, to move from passive object to active subject. The most important step is the claiming of her bodily power and integrating physical and (7.   ) strength to "make it" to the top, to "make herself a man." Because she is able to scale the pole when the other men cannot, it appears that her "power inheres in her blurred gender, in the fact of her cross-dressing, and not in *either* of her gendered identities."

06 Discussion/Writing/Presentation

次の問いかけについて，検討してみましょう。

① Many people say men are also discriminated against. Have you ever felt forced to act like a man?
② Nowadays some men do make up, work out, and shave their body hair. What do you think of that?

07 Further Discussion/Writing/Presentation

　右の画像は 1939 年に公開された『オズの魔法使／The Wizard of OZ』のものです。テクニカラー技術を用いて作られたこの映画の魅力は，今でも色あせてはいません。挿入歌として使われている「虹の向こうへ」(Over the Rainbow) も有名で，現在でも多くの歌手たちに歌い継がれています。

　この映画に主演しているのはジュディ・ガーランドです。ジュディは，たくさんのLGBTに支持されている「ゲイ・アイコン」(gay icon) でもあります。彼女がなぜゲイ・アイコンとして扱われるようになったのかについて調べて検討してみましょう。

　また，主人公ドロシーや彼女とともに行動する『オズの魔法使』の登場人物たちは，LGBT的人物の隠喩として捉えられることがあります。彼らが，どのような点でそのように言えるのかについても考えてみてください。

CHAPTER
06

Performing Meerkat and Warthog

00 *Warm-up*

1930 年代に導入されたハリウッド映画における Production Code 成立の経緯や歴史についてリサーチをし，簡潔に紹介しましょう。Rated G，Rated PG-13，Rated R が何を意味するのか，また，これらのレイティングシステムと Production Code との関係についても検討してみましょう。

01 *Vocabulary*

次の下線部の表現の意味を例文から推測し，下欄の語群①から訳語を選びましょう。また，その言い換えとして最適な英語表現を下欄の語群②から選びましょう。

例文	語群①	語群②
1. My teacher always **interpolate**s valuable comments into my report.		
2. When it comes to **diegetic** sound, we can associate the sound of heavy breathing, footsteps, creaky floors and slamming doors with scary scenes in movies.		
3. She has been one of the **mainstay**s of our research team in recent years.		
4. He was considered as something of a **maverick** in journalism.		
5. They were mimicking his boss's **flamboyant** hand gestures.		
6. He loved to be a **wisecracker** and was loved by all.		
7. Some of the girls were **rag**ging on her about her haircut.		
8. It is said that there are at least 37 plays in the Shakespeare **canon**.		
9. I was a social **outcast** at school because I had absolutely no interest in mingling with other students.		
10. It is said that having a **mentor** is one of the most important keys to success.		

語群①

(a) 中心となるもの，(b) 辛辣家・冗談を言う人，(c) 良き助言者，(d) のけ者・追放者，(e) 物語世界の，(f) からかう，(g) 独自路線を行く人・異端者，(h) 挿入する，(i) 大げさな・派手な，(j) 真作集・真作目録

語群②

(ア) a person or thing on which something else is based or depends, （ イ) a formal standard, rule, or principle, or set of these, that are believed by a group of people to be right and good, （ ウ) a person who makes a clever or sarcastic remark, (エ) an experienced and trusted adviser, (オ) to insert (something of a different nature) into something else, （ カ) of or relating to artistic elements that are perceived as existing within the world depicted in a narrative work, （ キ) to subject to a teasing, especially in an intense or prolonged way, （ ク) an unorthodox or independent-minded person, （ ケ) someone who is not accepted by the people they live among, or who has been forced out of their home, （ コ) behaving in a confident or exciting way that makes people notice you

02 Reading

Timon and Pumbaa are the "lovable" (Disney's characterization) comic sidekicks of Simba, the would-be Lion King. Timon and Pumbaa are in the mode of what Steve Seidman calls "comedian comedy," like the Marx Brothers, Martin and Lewis, Eddie Cantor, and Bob Hope and Bing Crosby: they are personas more than actors, addressing the audience directly, **interpolat**ing song-and-dance routines into the action and playing on their extra-cinematic selves with references to "showbiz" outside the **diegetic** universe of the film. This brings forth our first dilemma: Timon and Pumbaa subvert the "realistic" (in so far as animated characters can be realistic) performance style of the film. In general, animals in *The Lion King* behave like animals (albeit Disney animals): they walk on all fours, hunt (and kill) their prey, and are drawn in a fairly realistic style—with two important exceptions. They may wear the guise of meerkat and warthog, but Timon and Pumbaa have nothing to do with Africa. Said Nathan Lane: "My character, Timon, is more like a used-car salesman. Pumbaa and Timon are the low comedians. Kinda like two guys from Brooklyn who stop in the desert and became lovable cohorts." (A)The two guys from Brooklyn who show up in exotic locations and get into comic adventures are the **mainstay** of the road picture, best exemplified by Hope and Crosby, but also Laurel and Hardy, Martin and Lewis, and other comedy duos. Rather than realistic-acting animals performing a morality play set in prelapsarian Africa, Timon and Pumbaa are a classic comic duo dropped into a cartoon version of *Hamlet*. Timon is the crooning, egotistical wit, relying on verbal humor, puns, double entendres, wry looks, and double takes, while Pumbaa is the physical comedian, full of farts, belches, pratfalls, and visual gags centering on his ample belly and prominent rump.

Eric Smoodin points out that during the age of the classic cartoons, the 1930s and 1940s, animation stretched the boundaries of the Production Code because they were able to get away with double meanings and the kind of rude physical humor live actors would never be permitted to say or perform: "While cartoon sexuality was controlled by Hollywood's Production Code, animation also stretched the code or openly battled with it, in part for reasons related to studio competition, audience demographics, and historical context." Many "adult" characterizations and pieces of business were put into cartoons covertly, especially by **maverick**s at the Warners Studio and independents like Max Fleischer, while studio execs assumed they'd go over audience heads. Many of the best animators, marginalized by their parent studios, made shorts that reflected their own concerns and sensibilities, creating cartoons that are often startlingly political, bawdy, and satiric, much in the manner of a certain **flamboyant** meerkat and flatulent warthog.

Critics have noted the similarities between Timon and Bugs Bunny in design, attitude, and language. Both are **wisecracker**s (Bugs' catchphrase is "I'm a little stinker, ain't I?") and tricksters, and both are fluid in sexuality, regularly donning drag, singing show tunes, **rag**ging on notions of love and romance, and undermining relationships between other characters. But Timon, unlike the solitary Bugs, has a loyal "significant other": Pumbaa, his "bestest best friend." These two characters are obviously a same-sex couple—something singular in the Disney **canon**. They live together, they work together, and, long after their relationship has been affirmed, they raise a child together—a lion cub named Simba. Both characters are **outcast**s from their respective societies— Timon from the meerkat tunnels because, according to his "Diary," he broke into song while on guard-duty, and Pumbaa from his sounder due to excessive odor—but they find happiness together in their Oasis "dream home," a place isolated from the Pride Lands. Like many traditional film couples, they demonstrate that opposites certainly attract. Whereas Timon is a skeptic (perhaps mirroring his Shakespearean namesake, *Timon of Athens*), Pumbaa is sentimental and romantic. Pumbaa wants to adopt lion cub Simba because he's cute and helpless, ignoring that the cub will grow up to view his **mentor**s as prey, while Timon only agrees for purely selfish reasons—"Maybe he'll be on OUR side!"—but together they become loving and devoted "foster parents." When the adolescent Simba attempts to confront his destiny, the pair advise "You gotta put your behind in the past" (i.e., put your past behind you): it's the present that matters, not who you once were, but who you are now. (B)The question of whether your identity and responsibility is to yourself or to your family is a universal dilemma, but one especially relevant to gay people, who have often been rejected by their families and found new "families" among like-minded friends. (C)Obviously, the ultimate point of *The Lion King* is that Simba must realize where his true destiny lies and return to the Pride Lands and his responsibilities as king, but that message isn't "problem-free."

Nathan Lane (1956~)　アメリカの俳優。舞台俳優として活躍しているが，映画でも『バードケージ』(1996)，『プロデューサーズ』(2005) で2度ゴールデングローブ賞にノミネートされている。『ライオンキング』では声優を務めている。ゲイであることを公表している。
Timon　ティモン，砂漠に住むミーア・キャット。
Pumbaa　プンヴァ，ティモンの相棒のイボイノシシ。
guise　外観。
cohort　仲間。
prelapsarian　アダムとイブの堕落前の。
croon　小声で感傷的に歌う。
double take　後で気がついてハッと驚くこと。
wry look　しかめっ面。
pratfall　しりもち。
Bugs Bunny　バッグス・バニー，ワーナーのアニメに登場するウサギのキャラクター。
Hamlet　『ハムレット』1600 年から 1602 年ごろに書かれたとされるシェイクスピア原作の悲劇。幾度も映画化されているが，とりわけローレンス・オリビエの監督主演による 1948 年版はアカデミー賞作品賞を獲得している。
Production Code　ヘイズコードとも呼ばれるアメリカの映画検閲制度。1934 年から 1968 年まで施行され，映画の中での性や暴力描写などを規制した。
Max Fleischer (1883~1972)　マックス・フライシャー。アメリカのアニメーター，映画監督。『船乗りポパイ』(1933)『スーパーマン』(1941) などを制作。
Warner Studio　アメリカのエンターテインメント企業ワーナーブラザーズ。世界初のトーキー映画『ジャズ・シンガー』(1927) を制作したことで有名。

03 Comprehension Questions

（A）次の文が本文の内容と一致する場合は T，一致しない場合は F を選びなさい。

①	(T・F)	Timon and Pumbaa, the "lovable" comic sidekicks of Simba, entertain the audience like the Marx Brothers, Martin and Lewis, etc.
②	(T・F)	Timon and Pumbaa are depicted fairly realistically like other animals which walk on all fours and hunt their prey in the film.
③	(T・F)	Nathan Lane describes Timon as having an honest and reliable persona.
④	(T・F)	According to Eric Smoodin, the classic cartoons between the 1930s and 1940s never stretched the boundaries of the Production Code.
⑤	(T・F)	There are many similarities between Timon and Bugs Bunny; however, the latter has no duo partner.

（B）本文に関する次の問に答えましょう。

① What did many of the best animators, marginalized by their parent studios, do with their own concerns and sensibilities during the age of classic cartoons?

_____

② Why does Timon agree to adopt the lion cub Simba?

_____

③ When Simba is facing his destiny, what advice do Timon and Pumbaa give to him?

_____

04 Grammatical Structure

本文中の下線 A，B，C の文の主節における主部と述部を見分けましょう。

	主部	述部
下線 A		
下線 B		
下線 C		

05 Summary

次の文中の（　　　）に本文から適語を選んで書き込みましょう。

　　Rather than being realistic-acting animals performing a morality play set in prelapsarian Africa, Timon the meerkat and Pumbaa warthog behave like a comedian (1.　　　　　) from Brooklyn. Timon is the crooning, egotistical wit, relying on verbal humor, puns, double entendres, wry looks, and double takes, while Pumbaa is the physical comedian, full of farts, belches, pratfalls, and visual gags centering on his ample belly and prominent rump. Although both are (2.   ) from their respective societies, they find happiness in their Oasis "dream home," a place (3.   ) from the Pride Lands. They live and work together. As a same-sex couple, they become loving and devoted "(4.   ) parents" for lion cub Simba, the would-be Lion King. Critics point out the (5.   ) between Timon and Bugs Bunny in design, attitude, and language. However, Timon, unlike the solitary Bugs, has his "bestest best friend." According to Eric Smoodin, In the 1930s and 1940s animation (6.   ) the boundaries of the Production Codes by taking advantage of double meanings. Many of the best animators, (7.   ) by their parent studios, made shorts that reflected their own concerns and sensibilities, creating cartoons that are often startlingly political, bawdy, and satiric, much in the manner of a certain flamboyant meerkat and flatulent warthog.

06 Discussion/Writing/Presentation

次の問いかけについて，検討してみましょう。
① Do you think we should put our past behind us?
② Some LGBT people adopt and raise children, or have their own. What do you think of it?

07 Further Discussion/Writing/Presentation

　画像（左）の人物は，俳優業や歌手業だけでなく監督業なども含めて，幅広く活躍しているアメリカのスーパースターのバーブラ・ストライサンドです。彼女とLGBTとの関係について調べて検討してみましょう。
　また，画像（右）の人物は，イングランド出身の歌手・俳優のデヴィッド・ボウイです。ボウイの過去の発言などにも言及しながら，彼のセクシュアリティ（の変遷）についても考えてみてください。

Barbra Streisand photo: Allan warren

David Bowie

コラム②ジェンダー

　アンジェリナ・ジョリー主演の『マレフィセント』（2014）という映画をご存知でしょうか。マレフィセントといえば，『眠れる森の美女』の悪役として有名な魔女ですが，ディズニー製作のこの実写映画では彼女の視点から，お馴染みの物語が語り直されます。実際にはマレフィセントは心の優しい女性であったということ，また，キスでヒロインを目覚めさせるのが男性ではなく彼女であるところが，クラシックな『眠れる森の美女』とは大きく違っているところです。

　日本ではウーマンリブとよばれたラディカル・フェミニズムが起きたのは1960年代。この後，『シンデレラ・コンプレックス』『白雪姫コンプレックス』『眠りの森の美女にさよならのキスを』などこれらの物語の問題点を探る本が話題になり，女性も主体的に社会で活躍することが望まれるようになるにつれ，伝統的な女性ジェンダー（受動的・従順・他力本願）を踏襲するヒロインたちは批判に晒されることになりました。

　また2017年には，ハリウッドの大プロデューサー，ハーヴェイ・ワインスタインのセクハラ事件が明るみとなり，性的被害を告発する #Me Too 運動が堰を切ったように広がります。2018年のゴールデングローブ賞授賞式では，セクハラ撲滅を訴えるために女性スター俳優たちが一堂に黒いドレスで現れ，メディアで大きな話題となりました。2010年代になって，しばらくは下火に思えていたフェミニズム運動が再燃した感があります。

　もちろん，ジェンダーの被害者は女性だけではありません。男性も同様です。男性の場合は，肉体的・精神的に強くあることが期待されるので，常に虚勢を張っている男性は大勢います。とりわけ，アメリカはマッチョの伝統が強い国なので，日本以上にその傾向は強いです。また，男性のみに兵役を課している国は今でもありますし，学校での体罰や厳罰が与えられるのは圧倒的に男子であること，女性専用車両や映画のレディースデーなど女性に限定したサービスはあるのに男性限定のサービスがないこと，DVやセクハラなどの被害にあっている男性も多くいるのに男性の場合は被害を認めてもらえないことなど，たくさんの男性差別は存在します。

　これからの社会では，女性も男性も性の抑圧にとらわれない社会が期待されているのです。宮崎駿は，アメリカでも評価が高く，彼の率いるジブリはディズニーとも提携していますが，『もののけ姫』（1997）『千と千尋の神隠し』（2001）など，彼の作品では，大抵はアクティブな女の子が活躍し，心優しい男の子が登場します。そこが現代のジェンダーの流れに呼応しています。そこが，ジブリ作品が世界的に評価の高い理由の一つなのではないでしょうか。

Column

CHAPTER 07

"Hakuna Matata": A Problem-Free Philosophy? (1)

00 Warm-up

映画『ライオン・キング／ *The Lion King*』（1994年）の挿入歌 "Hakuna Matata"（スワヒリ語で「くよくよするな」の意味）が登場する場面に注目してみましょう。また，20世紀アメリカのコメディアンコンビ Laurel & Hardy についてインターネットで検索し，動画をチェックしてみましょう。そして調べたことを，PowerPoint などを使って，できる限り平易な英語で発表してみましょう。

01 Vocabulary

次の下線部の表現の意味を例文から推測し，下欄の語群①から訳語を選びましょう。また，その言い換えとして最適な英語表現を下欄の語群②から選びましょう。

例文	語群①	語群②
1. She pointed out the **contradiction** between his statements and his votes in the Senate.		
2. The memorial was built in 1872 under the **reign** of Queen Victoria.		
3. Her actions were motivated by **greed**.		
4. Religion played a **peripheral** role in the family's life.		
5. We were **overwhelm**ed by the number of applications.		
6. Over 60 of its members, including its leader, were arrested and accused of espionage, **subversive** activities and other crimes.		
7. All the patients were told to see their doctor for further treatment if their symptoms **persist**ed.		
8. There are many laws that impose certain **obligation**s on employers to protect the safety and health of employees.		
9. Prolonged question and answer sessions will eventually **elicit** the response the teacher is looking for.		
10. He showed a special **affinity** for the understanding and performance of the music of Bach.		

36

語群①

(a) 親近感・好み，(b) 転覆させる・破壊的な，(c) 持続・存続する，(d) あまり重要でない，
(e) 引き出す・誘発する，(f) 治世・統治，(g) 義務・責務，(h) 貪欲・強欲，(i) 圧倒する，
(j) 矛盾

語群②

(ア) a moral or legal duty to do something, (イ) to defeat completely, (ウ) intense and selfish
desire for something, especially wealth, power, or food, (エ) to continue to exist, (オ) strong
feeling that you like and understand someone or something, (カ) trying or likely to destroy or
damage a government or political system by attacking it secretly or indirectly, (キ) the period when
someone is king, queen, or emperor, (ク) not as important as the main aim or part of something,
(ケ) to draw forth (something that is latent or potential) into existence, (コ) a lack of agreement
between facts, opinions, actions

02 Reading

Which brings the next dilemma: Pumbaa and Timon's Oasis paradise is a site of major
contradiction and conflict between that intended message of *The Lion King* ("Remember who
you are") and the "problem-free philosophy" of "Hakuna Matata." (defined as "no worries, no
responsibilities"). The utopian pleasures of their non-sectarian enclave contrasts starkly with the
deadly desert from which they rescue Simba, the Elephant's Graveyard of the hyenas, and Pride
Rock itself, both before and after the **reign** of Mufasa: these are places Darwinian survival, of kill
or be killed, of jealousy, **greed**, and Machiavellian plots. In their safe and secure Oasis, Timon and
Pumbaa become surrogates for the murdered Mufasa and raise Simba to adulthood. (A)With their
humor, their charisma and their marketability, Timon and Pumbaa take on an importance not in
keeping with their **peripheral** status to the plot, and begin to **overwhelm** the "official" message
of the film, offering a **subversive** alternate reading. Pumbaa and Timon can be read as gay-
identified characters, living the closest thing to an "alternative lifestyle" to be found in the Disney
universe, and making that lifestyle a true option to the family values — heavy "moral" of the story.
Timon and Pumbaa embody the sensualist philosophy of "Hakuna Matata" and **persist** as self-
proclaimed "outcasts" in direct contrast to the Machiavellian family intrigues of the Pride Lands.
This **contradiction** comes across strongly in the narrative, but also in the characterizations and
marketing strategies of the film and later the television series, leaving the viewer (both child and
adult alike) with a contradictory message about whether your responsibility is to your family and
tradition, or to yourself and pleasure.

Obviously, as the plot plays out, Simba (and by implication the viewer of the film) is meant to
reject "Hakuna Matata" and return to his **obligation**s as the king of the Pride Lands. Timon and
Pumbaa aren't the most likely parental figures, but they can't have done such a bad job with their
foster son: Simba is able to defeat Scar and claim his birthright. The real dilemma is that "no
worries, no responsibilities" and "remember your responsibilities" are mutually exclusive concepts,
yet the film wants to have it both ways. King Mufasa (the resonant James Earl Jones) may be an

CHAPTER **07**

37

authoritative voice from heaven, but Timon and Pumbaa and the philosophy they represent are presented as more appealing, more fun, and much more marketable than the heavy-handed and ultimately violent path of Pride Rock.

The alternative lifestyle of Timon and Pumbaa **elicit**s the next dilemma of *The Lion King*. Do cartoon characters, especially those in traditional G-rated, child-centered animated features, have sexual identities? And if they do, how are those identities portrayed without actually suggesting sex acts? Sex is taboo in animated features (discounting underground films such as *Fritz the Cat*), especially at Disney, where the tradition of "family entertainment" is practically a fetish. So what do we make of Timon and Pumbaa? (B)British gay cultural critic Mark Simpson, writing about Laurel and Hardy, another comedian comedy duo beloved by children and adults equally and famous for their "harmless" and clean comedy style, states that in dealing with the non-erotic, almost pre-sexual relationship between Stan and Ollie, one must say that "Laurel and Hardy are not 'gay.' But they are not 'straight' either." Instead they exist in opposition to and in critique of heteronormative masculinity, and their confrontations with the adult world of regulation and repression are the basis of much of their comedy and our enjoyment of them. The skinny meerkat and the fat warthog partners function in much the same way as Stan Laurel and Oliver Hardy and extend a similar transgressive pleasure.

The very presence of Timon and Pumbaa in a children's animated feature offers a subversive reading within what is otherwise a determinedly conservative text. (C)In the imagery and narrative (drag, camp mannerisms, two males raising a child together), in the songs they sing (by gay superstar Elton John), in their vocal characterizations (by gay Broadway star Nathan Lane, one of Terrence McNally's stock company players and the star of *The Birdcage*, Mike Nichols' film version of French drag comedy *La Cage Aux Folles*, and Lane's frequent co-star, straight comic actor Ernie Sabella), and even in the marketing of products and a spin-off television series (Christmas ornaments of Timon in grass skirt and lei, Pumbaa's huge rump foregrounded on pillowcases), Timon and Pumbaa are decidedly queer characters. Their performance style, especially compared to that of the Pride Rock lions, is pure camp. They also display many of the stereotypical markers of "gayness" in American popular culture. They read as white and New York (at least when compared to supporting characters like the hyenas, voiced by Whoopi Goldberg and Cheech Marin, who read as urban and "Ghetto" and barrio!), are exaggerated in gesture and attitude, arch in expression and double entendre, overly emotional, and have an **affinity** for Broadway show tunes unusual in animals born and raised on the plains of Africa. As *New Yorker* reviewer Terrence Rafferty notes of Timon's "showstopper" performance: "The meerkat wisecracks constantly . . . and tends to get carried away when he sings and dances." In other words, Timon isn't just a drama queen, he's a theater queen!

Machiavellian マキャベリ流の，目的のためなら手段を選ばない。
James Earl Jones (1931~) ジェームズ・アール・ジョーンズ。アメリカの俳優。『ボクサー』(1970) でアカデミー賞主演男優賞ノミネート。2011 年アカデミー賞名誉賞受賞。声優としても活躍し，『スター・ウォーズ』のダース・ベイダーの声で有名。
G-rated G (general) 指定の，アメリカのレーティングは，G，PG，R，NC17 などに分かれるが，G は一般映画。
Fritz the Cat アメリカの漫画家ロバート・クラムによるアンダーグラウンドコミック。
Laurel and Hardy ローレル＆ハーディ。サイレントからトーキーの時代に活躍したお笑いコンビで，極楽コンビとも呼ばれている。Stan Laurel & Olivia Hardy のコンビ。
Terrence McNally (1938~) テレンス・マクナリー。『恋のためらい　フランキー＆ジョニー』(1991) などで知られる劇作家。ゲイの人物。
La Cage Aux Folles 『Mr. レディ　Mr. マダム』(1978)。フランスのゲイのカップルを描くコメディ。アメリカでも大ヒットとなりアカデミー賞 3 部門でノミネートされた。
Mike Nichols (1931~2014) マイク・ニコルズ。映画監督。アメリカ・ニューシネマを代表する名作『卒業』(1967) でア

カデミー賞監督賞受賞。『ワーキング・ガール』(1988)『バージニアウルフなんか怖くない』(1966)『シルクウッド』(1983)でも同賞にノミネート。

Ernie Sabella (1949~) アーニー・サベラ。アメリカの俳優。声優。

Whoopi Goldberg (1955~) ウーピー・ゴールドバーグ。アメリカを代表する黒人俳優のひとり。『カラーパープル』(1985)の主演でアカデミー賞にノミネート。その後,『ゴースト』(1990) で同賞助演女優賞を獲得。そのほか,『天使にラブソングを』などで活躍。

Cheech Marin (1946~) チーチ・マリン。アメリカの俳優, コメディアン。『カーズ』(2006) の声優としても知られている。

Barrio バリオ, スペイン語を話す人の地区。

showstopper ショーが一時中断されるような拍手喝采の名演技。

wisecrack 気の利いたことを言う。

Elton John (1947~) エルトン・ジョン。イギリスのミュージシャン。「僕の歌は君の歌」「キャンドル・イン・ザ・ウインド」「ダニエル」などのヒット曲を持つ世界的シンガーソングライター。ゲイであることをカミングアウトしている。『ライオン・キング』の主題歌「愛を感じて (Can You Feel The Love Tonight)」ではグラミー賞最優秀男性ポップボーカル賞とアカデミー賞歌曲賞を受賞。

03 *Comprehension Questions*

（A）次の文が本文の内容と一致する場合は T，一致しない場合は F を選びなさい。

① (T・F)	Simba is rescued by Timon and Pumbaa from Pride Rock.
② (T・F)	Timon and Pumbaa raise Simba in place of his father Mufasa, who was killed.
③ (T・F)	Simba eventually follows the "remember your responsibility" philosophy that the Pride Lands embody.
④ (T・F)	Disney movies are not very obsessed with the tradition of "family entertainment."
⑤ (T・F)	*The Birdcage* is a French movie which features Nathan Lane and was produced by Mike Nichols.

（B）本文に関する次の問に答えましょう。

① Which quality of Timon and Pumbaa helps overwhelm the main message of the movie, offering a different reading of the story?

_____

② Where does Simba have to return, giving up the "problem-free philosophy"?

_____

③ According to Mark Simpson, what is the basis of the comedy of Laurel and Hardy?

04 *Grammatical Structure*

本文中の下線 A，B，C の文の主節における主部と述部を見分けましょう。

	主部	述部
下線 A		
下線 B		
下線 C		

39

05 Summary

次の文中の（　　　）に本文から適語を選んで書き込みましょう。

In Pumbaa and Timon's Oasis paradise, there is a major contradiction between the intended message of the movie *The Lion King* and the "problem-free philosophy" of "Hakuna Matata." In their safe and secure Oasis, in stark (1.　　　　) to such places as the deadly desert and Pride Rock, Timon and Pumbaa raise Simba as surrogate parents. They offer a (2.　　　　) alternate reading to the movie. They can be read as a gay-identified couple, living an "alternative lifestyle." They (3.　　　) the problem-free philosophy, and as self-proclaimed "outcasts" they are free from the Machiavellian family intrigues of the Pride Lands. This leaves the audience with a contradictory message about whether your responsibility is to your family and tradition, or to yourself and pleasure. As the story progresses, Simba is to (4.　　　　) "Hakuna Matata" and return to his (5.　　　) as the king of the Pride Lands. Although "no worries, no responsibilities" and "remember your responsibilities" are mutually (6.　　　　) concepts, both of them are kept in the movie. Timon and Pumbaa and the philosophy they (7.　　　) are shown as more appealing, enjoyable, and even more marketable than the family values of the Pride Lands. Showing a variety of stereotypical markers of "gayness" in American popular culture, Timon and Pumbaa are certainly queer characters.

06 Discussion/Writing/Presentation

次の問いかけについて，検討してみましょう。

① In your opinion, what are traditional family values?

② Are there any animation movies or cartoons made as child-centered family entertainment in Japan?

	CHAPTER
	08

"Hakuna Matata": A Problem-Free Philosophy? (2)

00 Warm-up

ディズニー・アニメでは，有名な俳優が声優として起用されることがよくあります。たとえばロビン・ウィリアムズなどテキスト中に名前があがっている俳優が，俳優として登場している作品と声優として出演している作品についてリサーチし，平易な英語で発表してみましょう。さらに，エルトン・ジョンのバラード "Can You Feel The Love Tonight" も，歌詞と合わせて鑑賞しましょう。

01 Vocabulary

次の下線部の表現の意味を例文から推測し，下欄の語群①から訳語を選びましょう。また，その言い換えとして最適な英語表現を下欄の語群②から選びましょう。

例文	語群①	語群②
1. They both seemed quite **content** to let their parents do the talking.		
2. In fact, the emphasis on individual feelings **distract**s people from thinking about and caring for their communities		
3. He has been dating his boss's daughter on the **sly** for the past two years.		
4. We have to be careful about our **preconceive**d ideas misleading us.		
5. There are a number of **anomali**es in the present system.		
6. I just started playing the guitar, and the other people started **improvis**ing around me.		
7. We have **incorporate**d all the latest safety features into the design.		
8. It is said that eyes are more **eloquent** than lips.		
9. The movie is a brilliant **satire** on Hollywood.		
10. His visit to Soviet Union in 1927 produced a skeptical **critique** of the communist society.		

語群①

(a) 即興で作る，(b) 表情豊かな・雄弁な，(c) ひそかな・内密の，(d) 諷刺・あてこすり，(e) 変則・例外，(f) 組み込む・組み入れる，(g) 批判・批評，(h)（注意などを）そらす・紛らす，(i) 前からもっていた・いだいていた，(j) 満足して

語群②

(ア) clearly expressing or indicating something, (イ) a detailed explanation of the problems of something, (ウ) something that deviates from what is standard, normal, or expected, (エ) to take someone's attention away from what they are trying to do, (オ) acting or done in a secret or dishonest way, (カ) to include something so that it forms a part of something, (キ) happy and satisfied, (ク) formed before you have enough information or experience of something, (ケ) to perform without having planned or practiced something, (コ) a way of criticizing something such as the government or people's behavior by making fun of it in a clever way

02 Reading

As stated previously, Timon and Pumbaa are outcasts from their respective families (in a film where family is the key to one's identity), their social groups (meerkat tunnel and warthog sounder), and their species expectations (meerkat and warthog is not a pairing to be found in the "natural" order of things). In a world where mating and creating a family is primary, Timon and Pumbaa are **content** in their all-male enclave, complete with hot tub-like pool and insect buffet brunches. They also display a pronounced antipathy to heterosexual romance, as they prove when their adoptee, Simba, shows an interest in female interloper Nala, who, interestingly, can beat him up! And then there's Timon's famous hula drag. In the film, Timon puts on a grass shirt and lei, with a red hibiscus over his left ear, in order to **distract** the attacking hyenas, but the truth is that both Timon and Pumbaa revel in drag. In episodes of their television series *The Lion King's Timon and Pumbaa*, Timon donned a sarong, a pink waitress uniform, and another grass skirt and hibiscus, but this time with a string of pearls. Another continuing bit centered on Timon's various turns as a waiter ("My name is Timon; I'll be your waiter"), a modern updating of the old gay hairdresser stereotype. Pumbaa also appeared in drag during the series, most notably posing as Timon's wife to fool his mother so she won't realize that her son is living with his male warthog partner. Then there are statements made by Lane and Sabella during *The Lion King* publicity blitz, which range from **sly** innuendoes about their characters to forthright outing, including their joint interview with *The New York Times* and Lane's hilarious *Tonight Show* turn about gay, Jewish meerkats performing show tunes on the "Borscht veldt."

The characters of Timon and Pumbaa are also unusual for Disney in that they were created from the actors' Broadway personas, rather than being cast to fit **preconceive**d characters. Phil Harris in *The Jungle Book* and Robin Williams in *Aladdin* were two of only a handful of actors other than Nathan Lane and Ernie Sabella to ad lib many of their lines — and Lane and Sabella were unique in being allowed to record their lines together rather than singularly, as did the other voice actors. In this way Lane and Sabella put their individual stamps on the characterizations. Timon and Pumbaa were only created after Lane and Sabella, performing in the same musical on Broadway, arrived together to audition for the hyenas and began to joke around in the attitudes of their *Guys and Dolls* characters, which partly explains the stylistic **anomaly** of these streetwise, New Yorkese creatures. **Improvise**d dialogue inspired whole comic bits, such as Timon's hula, and even bodily functions were **incorporate**d into the narrative. One day Lane encouraged Sabella to make a rude noise into the microphone: "'We never thought they'd use it,' Mr. Sabella says, but the warthog's flatulence is now a running gag in the finished movie. 'They stole everything,' he says."

42

The characters were then animated (Timon by Mike Surrey and Pumbaa by Tony Bancroft) from videos of Lane and Sabella acting out their lines together, capturing their distinctive features, such as Sabella's fat, blustery cheeks, and Lane's **eloquent** eyebrows and anguished shoulder shrugs. (A)Characters voiced by actors with distinctive vocal styles and personalities, such as Timon and Pumbaa, Robin Williams' Genie, Phil Harris' Baloo, or Pat Carroll's Ursula, have often become the most memorable and beloved. Disney products are usually kitschy instead of campy, but it's interesting that the popular Cruella DeVil, Genie, and Ursula are all extremely camp creations, while Lane's Timon is the campiest of all, whether in drag, doing show tunes a la Jolson, or demonstrating the most flamboyant hand gestures since Jack Benny. (B)Lane, who was still publicly closeted at the time, but whose sexuality was widely known in New York theater circles, told the *New York Times* that "Timon is really me. . . . It's essentially me talking." When asked what specific aspects of his character the animators used, he replied, archly, "Oh, you know, staggering sensuality. Sexual danger." This is not what most Disney voice artists would be touting, but it's typical of the comments Lane and Sabella made in support of the film.

(C)If Lane and Sabella's campy interpretations influenced the development of their characters, then openly gay composer Elton John certainly impacted the way his music was used in the film, but to a different effect. The Academy Award winning ballad "Can You Feel The Love Tonight" was originally a comic parody of soft-focus movie interludes sung by Lane and Sabella. But John objected to the way *The Lion King* team had conceptualized his song as a **satire**. Said co-director Rob Minkoff: "Elton really felt it was part of the Disney tradition to keep the love song romantic," and the number was taken away from Timon and Pumbaa (except for the intro and tag ending) and given to Simba and Nala, revamped from a pointed satire to the kind of gushy ballad it had been intended to mock. The song is thus heteronormalized by playing it "straight," turning a comic **critique** of traditional Disney romance into an idyll of heterosexual awakening. It's possible that John, whose stock-in-trade is love songs for mainstream audiences, was uncomfortable with Lane and Sabella's camp send-up of his song (and by implication, his entire catalog) and therefore squelched their version. It's also possible that he recognized the power of Timon and Pumbaa's appeal, realizing that if the pair successfully undermine Nala, then Simba has no reason to question life at the oasis, let alone decide to reject it.

interloper　侵入者。
sarong　サロン。東南アジアや南アジアで，男性が腰に巻くロングスカート。
The Tonight Show **(1954~)**　アメリカの NBC で放送されているトーク番組。
Phil Harris (1904~1995)　フィル・ハリス。アメリカのコメディアン。
Robin Williams (1915~2014)　ロビン・ウィリアムズ。アメリカの俳優。コメディアンとしてスタートしたが，次第に演技派俳優として頭角をあらわし，『グッド・モーニング・ベトナム』(1987)，『いまを生きる』(1990)，『フィッシャー・キング』(1992) と 3 度主演男優賞にノミネートされた後，『グッド・ウィル・ハンティング』(1997) でアカデミー賞助演男優賞受賞。アルコール依存症を患い，自殺。
Guys & Dolls　1950 年初演のミュージカル。ブロードウェイでロングランになった。日本でも宝塚歌劇団で上演されている。マーロン・ブランドの主演で映画化され，日本では，『野郎どもと女たち』(1955) というタイトルで上映された。
streetwise　都会の環境で生き抜く技を持った。
flatulence　ガスがたまること。鼓腸。
Jack Benny (1894~1974)　ジャック・ベニー。アメリカのコメディアン。

03 Comprehension Questions

（A）次の文が本文の内容と一致する場合は T，一致しない場合は F を選びなさい。

① (T・F)	Timon wears a sarong, a pink waitress uniform, and a grass skirt and hibiscus in the movie.
② (T・F)	Robin Williams, cast as the character Genie in *Aladdin*, is known to ad lib his lines.
③ (T・F)	Most voice actors act out their lines individually rather than together/along with others.
④ (T・F)	Nathan Lane and Ernie Sabella, who voiced the characters in *The Lion King,* performed in the same Broadway show before the movie.
⑤ (T・F)	Elton John always liked the way his song was treated and used in the movie.

（B）本文に関する次の問に答えましょう。

① What kind of stereotype is implied in the character of Timon in episodes from the TV show?

_____

② In what way are the characters of Timon and Pumbaa unique in terms of creation for Disney movies?

_____

③ Who was originally meant to sing the song by Elton John in the movie?

_____

04 Grammatical Structure

本文中の下線 A，B，C の文の主節における主部と述部を見分けましょう。

	主部	述部
下線 A		
下線 B		
下線 C		

05 Summary

次の文中の（　　　）に本文から適語を選んで書き込みましょう。

　　Timon and Pumbaa are (1.　　　　　) from their families, and in a world where mating and creating a family is primary, they are (2.　　　　　) in their all-male enclave. They also display a pronounced (3.　　　　　) to heterosexual romance. In the film and during the following TV series, Timon puts on a hula costume in order to (4.　　　　　) the attacking hyenas, and Pumbaa also poses as Timon's wife to fool his mother. In fact, however, both of them enjoy drag very much. The characters of Timon and Pumbaa are also unusual for Disney in that they were created from the actors' Broadway personas, rather than being cast to fit (5.　　　　　) characters. Nathan Lane and Ernie Sabella, who voiced Timon and Pumbaa respectively, performed in the same musical on Broadway, and the characters were created only after that. The two voice actors are unique in ad-libbing many of their lines and recording their lines together rather than singularly. The characters were then animated from videos of the actors acting out their lines, (6.   ) their distinctive physical features and personalities, which made Timon and Pumbaa memorable and beloved. Improvised dialogue inspired such comic bits as Timon's hula, and even bodily functions were (7.   ) into the story. As Lane admitted, the voice artists' interpretations impacted the development of their characters in this movie.

06 Discussion/Writing/Presentation

次の問いかけについて，検討してみましょう。

① When you see a Disney movie dubbed in Japanese, how is it different from the original movie in English?
② Do you think songs inserted into a movie have impact on the story? Why or why not?

07 Further Discussion/Writing/Presentation

　画像（左）は，世界的に有名な歌手のエルトン・ジョンです。そして画像（右）はリアリティ番組『ル・ポールのドラァグ・レース／ RuPaul's Drag Race』でも活躍しているドラァグ・クイーンのル・ポールです。両者は，1993年に発表されたエルトンのアルバム『デュエット・ソングス／ Duets』で共演しています。

　エルトンは，同性婚をしたことでも知られていますが，イギリスで同性婚が合法化されるまでの歴史的経緯について調べて検討してみましょう。

　また，ル・ポールの番組にはドラァグ・クイーンが数多く出演し，大人気を博する長寿番組となっています。なぜ，この番組が視聴者の関心を集めているのかについても考えてみましょう。

Elton John　photo : Ernst Vikne

RuPau　photo : David Shankbone

CHAPTER 09

"Carnivores! Oy!": Disney and the Jewish Question

00 Warm-up

Disney の創設者 Walt Disney と CEO を務めた Michael Eisner のバックグラウンドについてリサーチしましょう。これら2人の人物を，それぞれの時代における家族の在り方にも言及しながら，英語で簡潔に紹介しましょう。

01 Vocabulary

次の下線部の表現の意味を例文から推測し，下欄の語群①から訳語を選びましょう。また，その言い換えとして最適な英語表現を下欄の語群②から選びましょう。

例文	語群①	語群②
1. This city has been an **amalgam** of different cultures for hundreds of years, each bringing their signature foods.		
2. The audience was overwhelmed by the singer's **over-the-top** outfit.		
3. A **feisty** grandmother chased a boy who tried to steal her purse.		
4. All the members of this club engage in lighthearted **banter** with each other.		
5. People know that fact that media sometimes **distort**ed the new.		
6. The mean host tries to **denigrate** his guests by reminding them of their past misdeeds in his talk show.		
7. One of the **subsidiary** organizations moved to Berlin from London last year.		
8. My sister was forced to sit through a long **diatribe** after coming home late at night.		
9. The movie I watched yesterday was full of **off-color** jokes.		
10. It is said that AI will **spawn** new businesses and industries in the future.		

語群①

(a) 歪める，(b) 傷つける・侮辱する，(c) 混合物，(d) 痛烈な非難・酷評，(e) 元気のいい，(f) いかがわしい，(g) 生む・引き起こす，(h) からかい・ひやかし，(i) 極端な・誇張された，(j) 従属する

語群②

(ア) active, forceful, and full of determination, (イ) to say things to make someone or something seem less important or good, (ウ) excessive or exaggerated, (エ) somewhat indecent or in poor taste, (オ) to report something in a way that is not completely true or correct, (カ) a forceful and bitter verbal attack against someone or something, (キ) the playful and friendly exchange of teasing remarks, (ク) mixture of different things, (ケ) connected with, but less important than, something else, (コ) to make a series of things happen or start to exist

02 Reading

Timon the Meerkat is not only gay-identified, but also New York and Jewish-identified: "Timon has a recognizable ethnicity... 'Sure, he's Jewish,' says Mr. Lane. 'Didn't you see him kiss the mezuza on the little tree?'" Nathan Lane, an Irish Catholic from New Jersey, instilled in his portrayal of Timon an **amalgam** of elements: his assertive stage persona as Nathan Detroit in *Guys and Dolls*, his gay leads in Terrence McNally comedic dramas *Love! Valour! Compassion!* and *The Lisbon Traviata*, the gay sidekicks and neighbors he played in films such as *Frankie & Johnny*. But he also stirred in more than a hint of New York Jewish humor. Lane delighted in ad-libbing phrases such as "Carnivores! Oy!" "So... Where ya from?" and the deathless "What do you want me to do? Dress in drag and do the hula?" in a voice with more than just a touch of Flatbush Avenue. Walt Disney himself was known to be anti-semitic in his personal life, if not in his business. Joked Lane of the traditionally conservative attitude at Disney: "I heard Walt wasn't very fond of the Jewish people. I'm sure he's spinning around in a refrigerator somewhere." So how much was Lane (in consort with Sabella) consciously subverting Disney norms? I would argue a lot, and that the writers and animators gleefully encouraged and nurtured his **over-the-top** interpretation of the role. Lane openly twitted Disney Producer Jeffrey Katzenberg, proclaiming Timon and Pumbaa's alternative sexuality on television and in print, and aligning the duo with various minority groups— Jews, gays, meerkats, people who sing out loud in public places—not usually associated with Disney products (but very often in Disney production and business!):

"Timon's a **feisty** little cheerful fellow," says Mr. Lane. "He has a very nice life. He and Pumbaa seem to have a very nice arrangement—though I couldn't say what the extent of their relationship is." The suggestion is obvious. Mr. Lane's grin is devilish. "I know what Nathan says about them," says Mr. Sabella, laughing. "'These are the first homosexual Disney characters to come to the screen.' Now that ought to get Jeffrey Katzenberg's attention. Hello!"

Katzenberg's response to the actors' teasing was reportedly, "I love it when you guys make fun of me"—but he didn't deny the possible validity of their remarks. (A)The irony of all this **banter** is that one of the attack points of the Religious Right in their campaign against *The Lion King* and Disney, is that the company and its products were part of a conscious "assault against Christianity" by Jewish CEO Michael Eisner and his minions, who had **distort**ed the American, Christian, and family-oriented fare served by "Uncle Walt" and replaced it with "Zionist sentiments" that not only **denigrate**d Christian values, but in films such as *The Lion King* and *Pocahontas*, "distort(ed) European-American history and disparag(ed) white America's racial-cultural heritage." During a mid-1990s debate about Hollywood "family values," Billy Crystal offered that, "When people say 'Hollywood Elite' what I really hear is 'Jew.'" So perhaps it's to be expected that beyond the

47

initial criticisms from the Left of the film as racist (the hyenas as Black and Hispanic stereotypes), sexist (the father and son relationship that marginalizes Sarabi and Nala), homophobic (Scar), were overshadowed by Right-wing Fundamentalist harangues against Disney itself. (B)*The Lion King* was a cog in a larger campaign of overtly sexual and homosexual propaganda linked to the release of the British independent film *Priest* in the spring of 1995 by Disney **subsidiary** Miramax, and was part of an on-going "Hollywood versus American Family Values" **diatribe** that called for the boycotting of all Disney products. As stated earlier, anti-abortion group The American Life League railed against "subliminal messages" hidden in Disney animated films, claiming that Disney cartoon features are full of erotic content and accus(ing) the head of the multimedia giant of peddling **off-color** products in the guise of family entertainment.... "I have no idea what (Disney CEO) Michael Eisner thinks he's doing. I have no way of knowing what their plan is for our kids. But they're making a fortune and these cartoons are filled with sexual imagery."

Judie Brown, president of the group, called for all Disney products to be removed from stores— a request Eisner and the Disney organization simply ignored. As *The Lion King* was released to video and DVD, **spawn**ed two sequels and a television series, and as *Pocahontas* (1995) continued Disney's animated feature success, the threatened boycott had little effect. But perhaps the greatest impact these campaigns had was less on business and more on the artistic process, where the creators seemed to delight in tweaking their critics. In the Timon and Pumbaa television series, as well as the second DVD sequel, *The Lion King 1 1/2*, the characters were made even more subversive to "Christian" norms. (C)Timon, still voiced by Nathan Lane, was gayer than ever and unmistakably Jewish, gaining a last name, Berkowitz, a stereotypical Jewish mother who calls him a "*meshugener*," and an Uncle Max who wants him to go into the family business.

mezuza　メズーザー。ユダヤ人の家屋やシナゴーグの門柱。
Flatbush Avenue　ブルックリンの通り。
Priest　『司祭』(1994) イギリス映画。ゲイの神父の苦悩を描く映画。ベルリン国際映画祭批評家連盟賞受賞。
peddle　ばらまく。
Michael Eisner (1942~)　マイケル・アイズナー。アメリカのテレビプロデューサー。ウォルト・ディズニー・カンパニー最高経営責任者を務めた (1984~2005)。

03 Comprehension Questions

（A）次の文が本文の内容と一致する場合は T，一致しない場合は F を選びなさい。

① (T・F)	Nathan Lane portrayed Timon only based on the characters he played in the films and dramas in the past.
② (T・F)	Nathan Lane adopted ad-libbed phrases in a voice with more than just a touch of Jewish New Yorkers.
③ (T・F)	It was known that Walt Disney clearly showed a strong dislike of Jewish people both at home and at work.
④ (T・F)	Anti-Disney boycott campaigns had a great impact on the company's sales.
⑤ (T・F)	Nathan Lane revealed that his mother would call him a "*meshugener*."

（B）本文に関する次の問に答えましょう。

① How did Nathan Lane notice that Timon was Jewish?

_____

② According to The American Life League, what hidden messages can be found in Disney animated films?

_____

③ Disney is known to be anti-semitic in his personal life. Who made fun of his attitude?

_____

04 Grammatical Structure

本文中の下線 A，B，C の文の主節における主部と述部を見分けましょう。

	主部	述部
下線 A		
下線 B		
下線 C		

05 Summary

次の文中の（　　　）に本文から適語を選んで書き込みましょう。

Timon the Meerkat is not only gay-identified, but also New York and Jewish-identified. Stirring in more than a hint of New York Jewish humor, Nathan Lane (1.　　　　) in his portrayal of Timon an amalgam of elements including his assertive stage persona as Nathan Detroit in *Guys and Dolls*, his gay leads in Terrence McNally comedic dramas *Love! Valour! Compassion!* and *The Lisbon Traviata*, and the gay sidekicks and neighbors he (2.　　　　) in films such as *Frankie & Johnny*. In addition, Lane openly twitted Disney Producer Jeffrey Katzenberg, proclaiming Timon and Pumbaa's alternative sexuality on television and in print, and aligning the duo with various (3.　　　　) groups—Jews, gays, meerkats, people who sing out loud in public places—not usually associated with Disney products. *The Lion King* was a cog in a larger campaign of overtly sexual and homosexual (4.　　　　) linked to the release of the British independent film *Priest* in the spring of 1995 by Disney subsidiary Miramax, and was part of an on-going "Hollywood versus American Family (5.　　　　)" diatribe that called for the boycotting of all Disney products. Despite anti-Disney campaigns, *The Lion King* was released to video and DVD, (6.　　　　) two sequels and a television series, and as *Pocahontas* continued Disney's animated feature success, the threatened boycott had (7.　　　) effect.

06 *Discussion/Writing/Presentation*

次の問いかけについて，検討してみましょう。

① What is your identity? Do you like or dislike to be identified by your birthplace, your school and other backgrounds?
② Do you think American family values have been distorted by Disney films?

07 *Further Discussion/Writing/Presentation*

　画像（左）は，歌手として1960年代から活躍しているだけではなく，1987年の映画『月の輝く夜に／Moonstruck』では，アカデミー主演女優賞を受賞するなど俳優としても活躍しているシェールです。シェールもまたゲイ・アイコンの1人であり，LGBT支援を行っていることでも知られています。

　画像（右）は，コメディアン・俳優としても活躍し，TV番組の司会としても知られているエレン・デジェネレスです。エレンの母は，娘であるエレンのレズビアンとしてのカミングアウト以降，LGBT支援活動に携わっています。ここでは日本を含めたLGBT支援団体とその活動について考えてみましょう。なぜそのような団体が必要なのでしょうか。

Cher

Ellen DeGeneres　photo : Alan Ligh

コラム③ LGBT

2015 年，アメリカ最高裁がついに同性婚を認めましたが，アメリカでは，同性愛に対する偏見はヨーロッパに比べて根強く，ヒラリー・スワンクが性同一性障害の女性に扮した『ボーイズ・ドント・クライ』（1999），ヒース・レジャーとジェイク・ジレンホール主演の男同士の恋愛映画『ブロークバック・マウンテン』（2004），実在のゲイの議員ハーヴェイ・ミルクを描く『ミルク』（2008）などでは，主人公は最終的に殺されてしまいます。日本ではマツコ・デラックスなど，ゲイの人がお笑いのネタになってしまいますが，殺されるという話はほとんど聞きません。アメリカの方がはるかに事態は深刻なのです。

LGBT という言葉は一般化してきましたが，L はレズビアン，G はゲイ，B はバイセクシャル，T はトランスジェンダーを指します。最近は LGBT に Q を加えるケースが出てきました。Q は，異性愛を規範とする社会に違和感を覚える性的マイノリティであるクィアを指す場合と，まだ自分の性に対して迷っているクエスチョニングを指す場合があります。その他にも無性愛者を指すアセクシャルも注目を浴びるようになってきました。また身体的に性別の判断が難しいインターセックス（半陰陽）の人も存在します。

2015 年，ジョニー・デップの娘がセクシャル・フルイディティであると公表して話題になりました。セクシャル・フルイディティとはセクシュアリティが流動的で変化していく人のことを指します。さらに，対物性愛（Object Sexuality）という愛の形も存在し，ライアン・ゴズリングが人形に恋する男を演じた『ラースとその彼女』は，その一例と言えるかもしれません。性は本当に多様です。100 人いれば 100 のセクシュアリティが存在するとも言われますし，「ストレート」と「ゲイ」のように単純に二分化することの方に問題があるようにも思えます。

映画でも，LGBT を扱うものは年を追うごとに増えているという感があります。スターたちも，ジョディ・フォスターやマット・ボマーなどカミングアウトする人が増えてきました。様々な人物が登場するアンサンブルものの映画では，ゲイが必ず 1 人は出てきます。例えば，『リトル・ミス・サンシャイン』（2006）ではスティーブ・カレル扮するおじさんがゲイという設定です。これはポリティカル・コレクトネスへの配慮がなされるようになってきたことの証拠です。

とはいうものの，マイケル・ダグラスとマット・デイモンがゲイを演じた『恋するリベラーチェ』（2013）は，あまりにもゲイ的な内容のため，映画会社が製作費を出してくれず，テレビ会社で製作され，アメリカではテレビで放送になったという経緯があります。

まだまだ世間の LGBT に対する偏見は根強いですし，ハリウッドスターは自分のイメージを気にするので，ゲイ役を演じるのには躊躇する人も多いはずです。従って，アメリカのLGBT ものはほとんど独立プロで作られ，無名の人を使っているケースが圧倒的です。ディズニーアニメも今のところ，主人公をゲイにしたものは思い当たりません。ディズニーがオープンにゲイを描くようになれば，その時こそが，LGBT の解放です。

CHAPTER

10

Mean Ladies: Transgendered Villains in Disney Films (1)

00 *Warm-up*

映画『ポカホンタス／ *Pocahontas*』（1994）で描かれている社会の時代背景をリサーチしましょう。また作品中の主要な登場人物のセリフやふるまいについても英語で簡潔に紹介しましょう。ウェブサイトやこれらの映画に関する書籍も参考にしながら，PowerPoint なども用いて，この作品に詳しくない人にもわかるよう要点を整理して発表しましょう。

01 *Vocabulary*

次の下線部の表現の意味を例文から推測し，下欄の語群①から訳語を選びましょう。また，その言い換えとして最適な英語表現を下欄の語群②から選びましょう。

例文	語群①	語群②
1. The manager thinks that the new leader of the union will be a formidable **antagonist**.		
2. Interdisciplinary studies are expected to cope with **disparate** ideas from different perspectives.		
3. He was dressed in white, which was almost **effeminate**.		
4. The old driver had his **disconcerting** habit of making a sharp turn.		
5. English sentences have to have an **overt** subject, except for the imperatives.		
6. The interests of filmmakers are not always **congruent** with those of sponsors for filmmaking.		
7. The AIDS epidemic further **stigmatize**d gays.		
8. Third countries must not **incite** an interested country to take military action.		
9. Some politicians oppose reform for **nefarious** reasons.		
10. The detectives finally obtained an **unequivocal** proof.		

語群①

(a) 異種の，(b) 明白な・決定的な，(c) 敵対者・競争相手，(d) そそのかして駆り立てる，
(e) 極度に邪悪な，(f) 顕在的な，(g) 適合する，(h) 女性のような，(i) 汚名を着せる，
(j) 狼狽させる・どぎまぎさせる

語群②

(ア) clearly different in quality or type, (イ) making someone feel anxious, confused, or embarrassed, (ウ) to describe someone or something in a very disapproving way, (エ) completely clear, (オ) displaying characteristics regarded as typical of women, (カ) to encourage someone to behave in a violent or illegal way, (キ) having the same size and shape as another, (ク) a person who you are having a contest, fight or quarrel with, (ケ) very wicked, (コ) observable or visible

02 Reading

"I want to watch one without a mean lady. "

That's what my three-year-old daughter said to me last spring, hoping I'd be able to find a Disney film for her to watch that didn't have a scary female character in it. Skeptically, already considering the overwhelming common knowledge of evil stepmothers in fairy tales, I investigated the ever-growing children's DVD pile in our home, setting aside film after film after film with yet another nasty **antagonist** in it. (A)But as I considered each Disney villain, especially in regard to his or her gendered characteristics, what I discovered truly gave me pause.

As we already know, most of the heroes and heroines of the beloved Disney film franchise are hyper-heterosexual—they fall in love, get married, and, as we understand it, live happily ever after, often singing, dancing, and acting googley-eyed right off into the sunset. Indeed, the primary characters reveal heterosexual goals by offering stereotypical and exaggerated portrayals of a traditionally gendered appearance (which then attracts an equally stereotypical character of the other sex). Later, these primary characters reinforce that identification through conventional behavior within their romantic relationships, as well as through their stated marital goals. These static identifications carefully craft a unified portrayal of happy heterosexism, which is clearly marked as the path to contentment and goodness.

But what I didn't realize until I fruitlessly examined that pile of DVDs was that the villains of Disney films also offer a distinct pattern via appearance and behavior—one that is quite **disparate** from the hyper-heterosexual heroes and heroines, and one that is disturbingly problematic. In contrast to the heterosexist leads, many of the villains display transgendered attributes—depicted as women with either strong masculine qualities or as strangely de-feminized, while the male bad guys are portrayed as **effeminate**, often complete with stereotypical limp-wristed affectation. These repeated motifs become even more **disconcerting** when they are coupled with the evil machinations for which, well, villains are known. (B)In other words, animated characters that offered transgendered characteristics that were positive or even simply neutral might be worth noticing to determine how or why that character related to others, especially the heterosexist leads; however, when gender-bending traits are assigned strictly to villains, then tension arises in terms of determining what, exactly, Disney is preaching so heartily and so frequently to its preschool choir.

The boundary-crossing of gender roles occurs in many Disney films, most notably in the Princess series, but also in animal-themed films as well. Specifically, several villainous female characters are masculinized in distinct ways, for example the stepmother and stepsisters in the Cinderella series and Ursula in *The Little Mermaid*. These females are certainly the "mean ladies" my daughter wanted to avoid. However, the gender-bending traits appear within male villains as well, as they are given **overt** (and even garish) feminine traits—some bordering on an implicit

CHAPTER 10

53

homosexual characterization. Specifically *The Lion King*'s Scar, *Aladdin*'s Jafar, and *Pocahontas*'s Ratcliffe also become transgendered villains, and eventually, my daughter grouped these characters as "mean ladies" too.

But Disney creating transgendered characters, of course, is not the issue, as doing so simply reflects society at large in a broader, more inclusive manner. As the organization Parents, Families, and Friends of Lesbians and Gays (PFLAG) indicates, "transgendered people are individuals of any age or sex who manifest characteristics, behaviors or self-expression, which in their own or someone else's perception, is typical of or commonly associated with persons of another gender." Thus, transgendered characteristics are those in which the sex of a person is not entirely **congruent** with their gender identity or actions. In other words, those who cross boundaries of traditional and/ or stereotypical gender identities may appear to be subtly, or even flamboyantly, transgendered.

However, when transgendered qualities are marked as only apparent in evil characters, then a **stigmatize**d standard of normative behavior is being created and promoted. Meredith Li-Vollmer and Mark E. LaPointe indicate in their article "Gender Transgression and Villainy in Animated Film," that "Gender is established and sustained by socially required identificatory displays; through interaction, gender is continually exhibited, and thus comes to be seen as "natural.'" "Likewise, when gender is exhibited in ways that have been identified socially as "unnatural," social stigmas or prejudicial evaluations may be **incite**d. Li-Vollmer and LaPoint continue, stating, "By performing gender outside of normative expectations, individuals may therefore draw into question much more than their gender: (C)In a culture with firmly naturalized constructions of gender, gender transgression may also cast doubt on a person's competence, social acceptability, and morality." In many of Disney's films, the villains portrayed are not only the bad guys in terms of their **nefarious** choices and desires, but also due to their so-called deviant behaviors via their gender performance. By creating only wicked characters as transgendered, Disney constructs an implicit evaluation of transgenderism, **unequivocally** associating it with cruelty, selfishness, brutality, and greed.

googley-eyed　ギョロ目で。
limp-wristed　「女々しい」「ホモの」という意味を持つ侮蔑表現。使用する際は要注意。
machination　陰謀、企み。
greed　貪欲。

03 Comprehension Questions

（A）次の文が本文の内容と一致する場合は T，一致しない場合は F を選びなさい。

① (T・F)	It is known that popular Disney films describe the primary characters as hyper-heterosexual, so that they typically prefer marriage of their own volition in the traditional style.
② (T・F)	Since the Disney films have a strong influence on children, even the villains in the films are brutal heterosexual characters.
③ (T・F)	Animal-themed films are distinct exceptions to those that masculinize villainous female characters, whom the author's daughter wanted to avoid.

④ (T・F)	If the sex of a person is not fully identical to their gender identity or actions, such characteristics are regarded as transgendered.
⑤ (T・F)	Gender performance is not a factor in making villains in many Disney's films evil characters.

（B）本文に関する次の問に答えましょう。

① What did the author do when his daughter said to him, "I want to watch one without a mean lady?"

_____

② Identify the examples of what the author's daughter grouped as "mean ladies."

_____

③ According to Li-Vollmer and Mark E. LaPointe what is considered to establish and sustain gender?

_____

04 Grammatical Structure

本文中の下線 A，B，C の文の主節における主部と述部を見分けましょう。

	主部	述部
下線 A		
下線 B		
下線 C		

05 Summary

次の文中の（　　　）に本文から適語を選んで書き込みましょう。

As we already know, most of the heroes and heroines of the beloved Disney film franchise are hyper-heterosexual—they fall in love, get married, and, as we understand it, live happily ever after, often singing, dancing, and acting googley-eyed right off into the sunset. However, when gender-bending traits are assigned strictly to (1.　　　　　), then tension arises in terms of determining what, exactly, Disney is preaching so heartily and so frequently to its preschool choir. The (2.　　　) of gender roles occurs in many Disney films, most notably in the Princess series, but also in animal-themed films as well. As the organization Parents, Families, and Friends of Lesbians and Gays indicates, "Transgendered people are individuals of any age or sex who manifest characteristics, behaviors or (3.　　　　　), which in their own or someone else's perception, is typical of or commonly associated with persons of another gender." Thus, transgendered characteristics are those in which the sex of a person is not entirely (4.　　　　) with their gender identity or actions. Meredith Li-Vollmer and Mark E. LaPointe indicate in their article "Gender Transgression and Villainy in Animated Film," that "Gender is established and sustained by socially required identificatory (5.　　　　); through interaction, gender is continually exhibited, and thus comes to be seen as "(6.   )". In many of Disney's films, the villains portrayed are not only the bad guys in terms of their nefarious choices and desires, but also due to their so-called deviant behaviors via their (7.   ) performance.

06 *Discussion/Writing/Presentation*

次の問いかけについて，検討してみましょう。

① Generally athletic types of men are portrayed as cool and loved by women in movies. Do you think it is a prejudice?
② Girls can wear both pants and skirts while boys cannot wear skirts. Do you think men will also wear skirts in the near future?

07 *Further Discussion/Writing/Presentation*

　画像は，クイーンというロックバンドのボーカリストとして，またバイセクシュアル／ゲイとしても有名なフレディ・マーキュリー（1991年没）です。このバンドが世界的にブレイクするきっかけとなったのは，デビュー間もない彼らの日本での熱狂的な人気でした。2018年には，このバンドを扱った映画『ボヘミアン・ラプソディ／Bohemian Rhapsody』も公開され，再び注目を集めることになりました。

　性的マイノリティでもある著名な人物を題材にしたメジャーな映画はこれまでにも制作されてきましたが，そのような映画は性的マイノリティに対する偏見をなくしうるのでしょうか，それとも偏見を強化してしまうのでしょうか。この問題について検討してみましょう。

Freddie Mercury　photo : Carl Lender

CHAPTER 11

Mean Ladies: Transgendered Villains in Disney Films (2)

00 Warm-up

映画『眠れる森の美女／*Sleeping Beauty*』（1959）で描かれているストーリーを要約し，英語で紹介しましょう。また，ウェブサイトや映画に関する書籍も参考にしながら，この作品を通して製作者が一番伝えたかったことが何かについて，自分なりの考えをまとめ，PowerPoint なども用いて発表しましょう。

01 Vocabulary

次の下線部の表現の意味を例文から推測し，下欄の語群①から訳語を選びましょう。また，その言い換えとして最適な英語表現を下欄の語群②から選びましょう。

例文	語群①	語群②
1. Mio's **aberrant** behavior worsened.		
2. Jason is hesitant about ridding himself of many **superfluous** belongings.		
3. The documentary TV program traced the **depiction** of kings from earliest times to the present day.		
4. Ladies cannot wait any more to be dressed in their finest **attire** at the ball,		
5. The powerful country would, they fear, only **reinforce** the power of allied countries.		
6. Diana is planning for the **transformation** of a school building into a multipurpose auditorium.		
7. There are quite a lot of things, either edible or environmental, that trigger off cell **proliferation**.		
8. Mr. Spicer spent thousands **renovat**ing his car, and his wife got mad at him.		
9. The motto of this institution is "Provide warm **nurtur**ing care for orphans."		
10. I know a professor who has **flirtation**s with a lot of students in and out of class.		

語群①

(a) 変形・転換，(b) 常軌を逸した，(c) 養育する，(d) 戯れ，(e) 良好な状態に戻す，(f) 描写・叙述，(g) 補強する (h) 必要以上の，(i) 増殖・蔓延，(j) 盛装させる・衣装

語群②

（ア）multiplication, （イ）to make something stronger, （ウ）unnecessary or no longer needed, （エ）to care for someone or something, （オ）behavior intended to arouse sexual feelings, （カ）a picture or a written description of it, （キ）changing something into something else, （ク）to repair and improve something, （ケ）unusual and not socially acceptable, （コ）clothes

02 Reading

Obviously, their complex gender identities are not what make these Disney villains wicked though. All of the villains act despicably: some bully and torment, while others are power-hungry or obsessive. As noted in *The Disney Villain*, "their behavior is **aberrant**, they are seemingly more colorful than the average person and they cause intense things to happen." In fact, "the character with evil intent supplies the strongest of contests throughout the performance." Their villainy creates the situation from which the hero and heroine must escape—and by which the heroes are most clearly defined. In other words, "we need evil to locate our good." The villains create the storyline–they have the plan, the methods, and the personality to problematize the situation— and typically that storyline also "disrupt[s] and frustrate[s] heterosexuality's dominance" by antagonizing the happily-ever-after of the heroes and heroines. The princesses and their princes simply react to those plans, allowing their "goodness" to be shown via their reactions to the bad guys. And yet, these evil actions or desires have very little to do with their gender-bending portrayals—in fact they are **superfluous** to them. However, it is the noxious combination of transgendered characteristics with these characters'evil plots and exploits that makes this spicy blend so unpalatable once clearly recognized–and yet, that combination goes unrealized by most viewers, whether child or adult–accepted without examination, reinforcing the heterosexism of current contemporary culture.

(A)To best understand the villains' complicated gender identities, it's first important to examine the high profiles of the main characters to which they are contrasted. The dominant heterosexuality of the heroes and heroines is significant because it helps display the stark dissimilarity of the villains' transgendered **depiction**. For many of the leading male and female characters, their heterosexuality is illustrated first through their appearance. Strong, commanding princes and other handsome male leads are coupled with young beautiful women, many with long hair and most in flowing **attire**, which emphasizes their hour-glass figures.

Disney princesses are most frequently shown wearing one main outfit, which was created to **reinforce** their heterosexuality. All of their clothes are form-fitting, with a few of them also revealing cleavage. Sleeping Beauty, Belle, and Tiana all bare the tops of their breasts via ballroom gowns with low necklines. Similarly, Cinderella wears low, scoop-necked

dresses that emphasize a small waist and rounded bust. In Pocahantas, the lead character wears a one-shouldered mini-dress, which exposes both ample cleavage and long legs. Jasmine wears an off-the-shoulder bra with flowing, transparent harem pants, which linger several inches below her navel, and Ariel wears only shells on her breasts, while the top of her mermaid tail similarly dips intriguingly low beneath her belly button. In making each heroine's outfit form-fitting, especially around her breasts, waist, and hips, Disney accentuates the ideal heterosexual female figure to viewers: curvy breasts and hips, an unrealistically small waist—and tight apparel to show it all off.

(B)In fact, critiquing Pocahontas's appearance in more depth suggests a concerted effort to make her hyper-heterosexual. While Nakoma, Pocahontas's best friend, wears a revealing mini-dress too, the difference in their appearance is considerable. Both women have tiny waists; however, Pocahontas has extremely large breasts in comparison to Nakoma's more modest bosom, emphasizing Pocahontas as the female lead. Discussing the dubious historical accuracy of transforming Pocahontas into a clearly much older (and sexier) woman than the actual Powhatan princess of American lore, Mark I. Pinsky indicates that "the **transformation** of a preteen ... to a nubile babe in off-the-shoulder buckskin, with pouty, collagen lips" should not be overlooked. In fact, supervising animator Glen Keane explained "Jeffrey Katzenberg (then the chairman of Walt Disney Studios) said he wanted her to be the most idealized and finest woman ever made." Clearly, like others in the Disney Princess series, Pocahontas's appearance heavily markets the heterosexual feminine vision.

(C)A **proliferation** of stereotypically female behaviors, such as standard finishing school traits, pre-occupations with domestic work, as well as an affinity for animals also mark many of the princess characters as ultra-feminine, at least as Disney defines it. Even with no apparent dancing lessons, Sleeping Beauty, Cinderella, Belle, and Tiana are light on their feet as they dance with their respective Princes. Of course, all of the princesses sing well since each Disney film is a musical, but Ariel also has the lead singing role in the production which starts the film. Both Cinderella and Tiana show amazing grace and poise, with Cinderella being able to balance three tea trays (one on her head!) while going upstairs to serve her stepfamily, and Tiana similarly balancing a variety of plates and trays while waitressing. Snow White, Cinderella, and Sleeping Beauty clean houses while smiling, seemingly enjoying the work. Likewise Tiana demonstrates a strong work ethic to clean and **renovate** an abandoned building so as to become a chef for her new restaurant. The princesses also have numerous animal friendships, which they **nurture** maternally. Snow White, Cinderella, and Sleeping Beauty befriend forest animals and house mice, while Ariel befriends fish, crabs, and a crane. Likewise, Jasmine's "only friend" before she leaves the palace is her huge pet tiger. Tiana actually becomes a frog, and is then happily assisted by numerous swamp bugs and creatures. While Belle is primarily friendly with the people of the castle who were transformed into furniture and household goods, these characters act in similar ways to the animal friends of other princesses. These traditional behaviors, used as standardized Disney tropes of femininity, signal to viewers that the princesses are all heterosexual, maintaining goals of marriage, domestic life, and family.

Disney heroes typically play a smaller part than their princess; however they too embody heterosexual characteristics in their appearance and behavior, thus providing male balance to the film. Taller than each respective princess, broad-shouldered, square-jawed, and muscular, their attributes become standardized heterosexual male physical characteristics. They also participate in "manly" activities, such as horseback riding, hunting, sailing, sword-fighting, and even hand-to-hand combat, when necessary. Additionally, they share two crucial characteristics: they fall in love with the heroine immediately, and they rescue her when needed. For example, Cinderella and her Prince sing, "So This Is Love" as they dance for the first time, while Ariel falls in love with Prince Eric upon seeing him from afar on his boat. Thus, the appearance and behavior of the male-female leads emphasize their heterosexuality, and that **flirtation** is rewarded: most of the princesses marry their prince at the end of the film, underscoring the goals of heterosexual attraction, love, marriage, and eventually, family.

despicably 侮辱する態度で。
bully いじめる。
torment 悩ます。
obsessive 強迫的。
noxious 有害な。
hour-glass figure 砂時計のような姿（腰をコルセットで締めたドレスを着ているので，砂時計のような姿となる）。
scoop neck ドレスの半月状に深く切られた襟ぐり。
off-the-shoulder 肩を覆っていない。
harem pants 女性用のゆったりしたズボン。
belly button へそ。
nubile 年ごろの，性的魅力のある。
finishing school 花嫁学校。

03 *Comprehension Questions*

（A）次の文が本文の内容と一致する場合は T，一致しない場合は F を選びなさい。

① (T・F)	The wicked nature of many Disney villains can be ascribed to other factors than their complex gender identities.
② (T・F)	The depiction of transgendered characteristics is manipulated to create a contrast with the dominant heterosexuality of heroes and heroines.
③ (T・F)	Most Disney princesses are characterized as wearing sexy dresses exaggerating their breasts, because they have an appealing power to heterosexual male heroes.
④ (T・F)	Stereotypical female behavior, such as dancing, singing, befriending forest animals, is important for princesses because heterosexuality is the goal of their life.
⑤ (T・F)	Although the role of Disney heroes' manly characteristics is relatively small, they contribute to approving of heterosexuality.

（B）本文に関する次の問に答えましょう。

① What is the role of the princesses and their princes in reacting to villains' evil plots?

_____

② What is implied in Jeffrey Katzenberg's comment on the appearance of Pocahontas as "the most idealized and finest woman ever made?"

_____

③ Identify two characteristics that heterosexual heroes commonly have.

_____

04 *Grammatical Structure*

本文中の下線 A，B，C の文の主節における主部と述部を見分けましょう。

	主部	述部
下線 A		
下線 B		
下線 C		

05 *Summary*

次の文中の（　　　）に本文から適語を選んで書き込みましょう。

　As noted in *The Disney Villain*, "Their behavior is (1.　　　　), they are seemingly more colorful than the average person and they cause intense things to happen." In fact, "The character with evil intent supplies the strongest of contests throughout the performance." Their villainy creates the situation from which the hero and heroine must (2.　　　　)—and by which the heroes are most clearly defined. Disney princesses are most frequently shown wearing one main outfit, which was created to reinforce their (3.　　　　). A proliferation of stereotypically female behaviors, such as standard finishing school traits, pre-occupations with domestic work, as well as an affinity for animals also mark many of the princess characters as ultra-feminine, at least as Disney defines it. Of course, all of the princesses sing well since each Disney film is a (4.　　　　), but Ariel also has the lead singing role in the production which starts the film. While Belle is primarily friendly with the people of the castle who were (5.　　　　) into furniture and household goods, these characters act in similar ways to the animal friends of other princesses. These traditional behaviors, used as standardized Disney tropes of (6.　　　　), signal to viewers that the princesses are all heterosexual, maintaining goals of marriage, domestic life, and family. Disney heroes typically play a smaller part than their princess; however they too (7.　　　　) heterosexual characteristics in their appearance and behavior, thus providing male balance to the film.

06 *Discussion/Writing/Presentation*

次の問いかけについて，検討してみましょう。

① Do you think parents should allow children to watch whatever they want?

② Why do you think many films include sexually explicit scenes?

CHAPTER 12	Mean Ladies: Transgendered Villains in Disney Films (3)

00 Warm-up

映画『シンデレラ／Cinderella』（1950），その続編の OVA『シンデレラⅡ／Cinderella II: Dreams Come True』（2002），『シンデレラⅢ 戻された時計の針／Cinderella III: A Twist in Time』（2007）の主要な登場人物と物語のあらすじについてリサーチをし，英語で簡潔に紹介しましょう。インターネットやこれらの映画に関する書籍を活用し，PowerPoint なども用いて，オーディエンスのことも考慮しながらわかりやすく発表することを心がけましょう。

01 Vocabulary

次の下線部の表現の意味を例文から推測し，下欄の語群①から訳語を選びましょう。また，その言い換えとして最適な英語表現を下欄の語群②から選びましょう。

例文	語群①	語群②
1. In this point, the American farmer appears to be very similar to his Chinese **counterpart**.		
2. The company's policy is to **adhere** to the facts and get accurate information from third party experts.		
3. The company combines traditionally **masculine** and feminine qualities in its products.		
4. In the year, the Trudeau government pledged to spend $650 million on sexual and **reproductive** health and rights.		
5. There was something about him vaguely **reminiscent** of an octopus.		
6. He could not **contemplate** the possibility of a life entirely without her.		
7. She is shy around those she does not know. She is somewhat **awkward** as a public speaker.		
8. The e-Vote system must cope with possibilities of electoral chicanery: **impostor**s, double voters, and enforcers.		
9. A few minutes later he heard the **clumsy** movements of his son rushing out of the room.		
10. "The fact that you take care of me doesn't give you the right to **humiliate** me," he said.		

語群①

(a) 男性的な，(b) 夢想する，(c) 固く守る，(d) 詐称者，(e) 思い出させる，(f) 生殖の，
(g) ぶかっこうな，(h) 対応するもの（人），(i) 不器用な，(j) 恥をかかせる

語群②

(ア) having qualities or appearance considered to be typical of men traditionally，(イ) causing uneasy embarrassment，(ウ) relating to or effecting the process of producing babies or young animals，(エ) closely follow (a particular rule, agreement, or belief)，(オ) to think about something in the future，(カ) someone or something that corresponds to someone or something else in a different place or situation，(キ) moving or doing things in a careless way and likely to upset someone，(ク) to make someone feel ashamed or foolish by injuring their dignity and pride，(ケ) suggesting something by resemblance，(コ) a person who pretends to be someone else in order to trick people

02 Reading

Even Disney's animal royalty depict hyper-heterosexuality in similar ways as their human **counterparts**. In *The Lion King*, King Mufasa and his mate, Sarabi, are happily married, with their newborn cub Simba introduced at the beginning of the film. The lion couple **adheres** to traditional gender roles in raising their son: Mufasa shares his wisdom with Simba about their ancestors and Simba's as the future king, while Sarabi ensures Simba is clean, fed, and obedient. Soon, viewers find out Simba and his childhood friend, Nala, are betrothed, asserting another standard heterosexual goal of marriage even though they are only young cubs. When the two lions meet again as young adults, they immediately fall in love, reassuring viewers that they will willingly marry each other to fulfill the heterosexual agenda. (A)Clearly, Disney's royalty, whether human or animal, portray a safely traditional heterosexual view of the world, which offers a clear contrast to the complexity of the transgendered villains who are introduced slightly later in each film.

Dramatic and daring, the villains often outperform their heterosexual rivals, setting up a transparent comparison between "normative" and "deviant" gendered behaviors, but also connecting the villains' transgenderism with sarcasm, selfishness, cruelty, greed, and brutality. Many of the female Disney villains are subtly **masculine**—their faces, body shape, and behavior lend "mannish" traits to their characters. In portraying them this way, the villains contrast sharply with the ultra-feminine princesses. This allows my daughter, one of Disney's intended audience, to recognize more easily who is "good" in these films—and who is not. But it also gives a bewildering message regarding difference, suggesting that real transgendered people are extremely dangerous and to be avoided at all costs.

Lady Tremaine, the stepmother in the Cinderella series, and her two daughters, Drizella and Anastasia, are supposed to be mean--viewers already know this from the Grimms' fairy tale on which Disney's film is based. Likewise, various versions of the tale exclaim their ugliness. But the way Disney portrays their villainy via transgendered characteristics is what is fascinating-and disturbing.

In contrast to the lithe feminine figure of Cinderella, both stepsisters are decidedly masculine. Neither stepsister has breasts as both girls are flat-chested, appearing, in fact, square-bodied, with no difference in width between their chest and their waist. The complete absence of their breasts makes them appear both mannish and non-reproductive, contrasting strongly with Cinderella and other princess figures, with their heterosexual **reproductive** agendas. Likewise, instead of the gently scooped or deep necklines of the princesses, (B)Drizella and Anastasia head off to the ball wearing squared-off necklines, which accentuates their flat chests. Likewise, their dresses both have extremely large bustles, emphasizing their lack of a female figure and awkwardness.

Additionally, the stepsisters' faces are boyish and considered unfeminine by most others. With scowling brows, large round eyes (and even rounder noses), plus a jowly lower jaw and neck, their faces are **reminiscent** of Disney's Pinocchio or the Lost Boys of *Peter Pan*. As he watches the stepsisters awkwardly engaging his son, the King negatively shakes his head and hands vigorously, saying, "I give up. Even I could not expect the boy to...," implying that both stepsisters are just too ugly for him to even **contemplate** his son marrying them. Even before they are allowed to try the glass slipper on, the Duke winces at the sight of them. Bell, Haas and Sells argue that that the two stepsisters cross the gender line completely, appearing male: "with their flat chests, huge bustles, and **awkward** curtsies, [the stepsisters] could as well be read as comic drag acts in this balletic fantasy." Clearly, their ugliness is really maleness costumed as female.

(C)Both stepsisters, and Anastasia in particular, are further associated with masculinity via their large feet, which contribute to their extreme clumsiness, ensuring a safe distance from princess poise. Throughout the original film, the stepsisters' feet are shown to be at least three times as large as Cinderella's, sometimes taking up the entire screen. Whether lying in bed, curtsying to the prince, or being fitted for the slipper, the stepsisters' feet are massive and fleshy. In contrast, the Grand Duke shows just how tiny the glass slipper is that fits Cinderella—it fits inside his palm with the toe of the shoe as small as his fingers. In the first Cinderella film, Anastasia tries on Cinderella's tiny glass slipper, but manages only to get her big toe inside. In the third Cinderella film, her fleshy foot actually fits (much to the visible dismay of the Grand Duke), via Lady Tremaine's evil use of the Fairy Godmother's wand. Astonished and thrilled, Anastasia immediately undermines this feminine quality by displaying ungainliness: Anastasia crashes around the room, twirling the cat while screeching, "It fits!" Lady Tremaine even catches her daughter's legs mid-cartwheel, allowing Anastasia's dress to fall over her head, revealing her bloomers, before Anastasia collapses with her rump in the air. In effect, this scene ensures that preschool viewers understand Anastasia as the bumbling, awkward **impostor** that she is: although the shoe fits, she is not a true princess.

Further, the stepsisters exhibit a range of behaviors that mark them as masculine. When waiting to be introduced to the Prince, the girls are gawky in their presentation, Drizella also making the mistake of bowing, instead of curtsying to the Prince. The mistake makes her appear even more mannish, as she chooses a traditionally male form of presentation, bolstering the concept that she is not really a girl at all. Likewise, both stepsisters are **clumsy** and awkward, tripping over themselves and others constantly--Anastasia even **humiliate**s herself by stepping on the Prince's feet a record seven times when they dance in Cinderella III. The sisters also physically fight with each other, emphasizing their boyishness by participating in still more traditionally male behavior.

Cinderella's ever-present gracefulness contrasts with their lack of femininity at every awkward sashay and piercing melody (in fact, Cinderella even giggles demurely about their lack of singing talent).

cub （肉食動物の）子，幼獣。
sarcasm 皮肉，当てこすり。
lithe しなやかな。
bustle 腰当て。
scowling 顔をしかめる。
wince ひるむ，たじろぐ。
sashay 片方の足でリードしながら，早く滑るように進むステップ。
demurely 控えめな態度で。

03 Comprehension Questions

（A）次の文が本文の内容と一致する場合は T，一致しない場合は F を選びなさい。

① (T・F)	Animal characters in Disney's movies are often different from human ones concerning gender roles.
② (T・F)	Mufasa plays a major role in raising his son as the future king, which makes him a traditional father.
③ (T・F)	The villains in Disney's movies reflect a traditional heterosexual view of the world.
④ (T・F)	Transgendered characteristics of the female Disney villains are connected with sarcasm, selfishness, cruelty, greed, and brutality.
⑤ (T・F)	In the movie, Cinderella's tiny glass slipper is used to show a general belief that women who have small feet are feminine and qualified as real princesses.

（B）本文に関する次の問に答えましょう。

① Who play a traditional parent role in the Lion King?

_____

② In the Cinderella movies, what makes the heroine's stepmother and stepsisters transgendered?

_____

③ What are the typical heterosexual characters like in Disney's movies?

_____

04 Grammatical Structure

本文中の下線 A，B，C の文の主節における主部と述部を見分けましょう。

	主部	述部
下線 A		
下線 B		
下線 C		

05 Summary

次の文中の（　　）に本文から適語を選んで書き込みましょう。

Disney's heroes and heroines, whether human or animal, portray a safely traditional (1.　　　) view of the world, which offers a clear contrast to the (2.　　　) of the transgendered villains. The villains often outperform their heterosexual rivals, setting up a transparent comparison between "normative" and "deviant" (3.　　　) behaviors. But the villains' transgenderism is connected with sarcasm, selfishness, cruelty, greed, and brutality. In portraying them this way, the villains contrast sharply with the ultra-feminine princesses. This allows young children to (4.　　　) more easily who is "good" and who is not in these films. But it also gives a (5.　　　) message regarding difference, suggesting that real (6.　　　) people are extremely dangerous and to be avoided at all costs. The stepmother in the *Cinderella* series, and her two daughters are supposed to be mean--viewers already know this from the Grimms' fairy tale on which Disney's film is based. But the way Disney portrays their villainy via transgendered characteristics is what is fascinating-and disturbing. In contrast to the feminine figure of Cinderella, both stepsisters are decidedly masculine. Cinderella's ever-present gracefulness contrasts with their (7.　　　) of femininity.

06 Discussion/Writing/Presentation

次の問いかけについて，検討してみましょう。

① Do you think that it is possible to succeed in animation movies which have transgendered princesses?
② What do you think is important to improve your understanding of people who are different from you in sexual orientation?

07 Further Discussion/Writing/Presentation

　　マドンナ（画像左）とレディ・ガガ（画像右）はともに，同性婚の擁護などLGBTの権利拡大を支持しており，新旧のゲイ・アイコンでもあります。
　　日本の歌手や俳優でも公にLGBT支援を行っている人はいるのでしょうか。また，日本にもゲイ・アイコンとして注目される存在はいるのでしょうか。いるとすれば，彼／彼女たちはなぜゲイ・アイコンとみなされるようになったのかについても調べて検討してみましょう。

Madonna　photo : JD Urban　　　　Lady Gaga　photo : Lee Chu

コラム④多様性を認め合う社会へ

　2016年のアカデミー賞では，白人偏重主義がバッシングされました。前年に続いて，2年連続で演技賞（主演男優・主演女優・助演男優・助演女優）の候補者が全員白人という事態が起きたからです。

　その反動もあってかその翌年2017年のアカデミー賞では『ムーンライト』が作品賞を受賞しました。2015年，『グローリー　明日への行進』で監督賞の有力候補と見做されていた，エイヴァ・デュヴァネーがノミネートすらされなかったときは，彼女が黒人でしかも女性であるがゆえの二重の差別だと騒がれたのですが，『ムーンライト』は，黒人でしかもゲイという二重の差別を受けている男性を主人公にしたもので，これに賞が行ったことでポリティカルコレクトネスの調整がなされたといっていいかもしれません。

　このテキストで問題にされているのは，主として性の問題（ジェンダーとLGBT）ですが，これと並んで必ず議論されるのが階級と人種の問題です。アメリカは貧富の差が激しく，民主主義社会とは言うものの，大きな階級差が存在していることは，ポール・フアッセルの『階級「平等社会」アメリカのタブー』という本の中で語られています。一方で，様々なエスニシティーが存在する国でもあるため人種問題も深刻です。黒人問題の映画はアカデミー賞作品賞を獲得した『それでも夜は明ける』（2014）など枚挙にいとまがありませんが，他にも，ユダヤ系は『アニー・ホール』（1977）などウッディ・アレンの一連の映画，ヒスパニックはミュージカルの名作『ウエスト・サイド物語』（1961），アイルランド系はクリント・イーストウッド監督の『ミリオンダラー・ベビー』（2004），イタリア系は『ゴッド・ファーザー』（1972）などマフィアもので描かれてきています。

　さらに，最近では身体障がいや発達障がいなどにも世間の関心が向かうようになりました。階級・人種・障がい・性（ジェンダーやLGBT），いずれも差別につながる事柄です。アメリカは多様な人がともに生活している国なので，様々な差別が重層的に繰り広げられるのです。エミネムが主演した『8 Mile』（2003）はラップの世界での白人男性差別を描くものですが，白人で男性だから必ずしも権力を握るわけではないことが訴えられており，差別の問題は複雑です。

　ディズニーのアニメ『ズートピア』（2016）には，様々な動物が登場しますが，これは人間を動物に置き換えて，多様性のメタファーとして描いた映画と言えるでしょう。この映画の動物たちのように，様々な人々がお互いの相違を認め合い，障がいも性的指向も全てその人の個性だと思うことのできるような世の中になれば，それこそユートピアです。多様性は21世紀のキーワードと言っていいでしょう。ディズニーアニメでも，『アナと雪の女王』（2013）はLGBTやフェミニズムの角度からも捉えることができますし，『モアナと伝説の海』（2016）ではポリネシア，『リメンバー・ミー』（2017）ではメキシコの文化が描かれます。ディズニー映画は着々と進化を遂げていると言えます。

CHAPTER

13

Mean Ladies: Transgendered Villains in Disney Films (4)

00 *Warm-up*

映画『リトル・マーメイド／ *The Little Mermaid*』（1989）の主要な登場人物と物語のあらすじについてリサーチをし，英語で簡潔に紹介しましょう。インターネットやこれらの映画に関する書籍も活用し，PowerPoint なども用いて，オーディエンスのことも考慮しながらわかりやすく発表することを心がけましょう。

01 *Vocabulary*

次の下線部の表現の意味を例文から推測し，下欄の語群①から訳語を選びましょう。また，その言い換えとして最適な英語表現を下欄の語群②から選びましょう。

例文	語群①	語群②
1. Social and political pressures often **solidify** national identities.		
2. If some statements, beliefs or practices are claimed to be scientific but are compatible with the scientific method, they can be called **pseudo**-science.		
3. The research shows that the **divergence** between the incomes of the rich and the poor countries is increasing.		
4. Dogs running loose are a **menace**, especially to small children.		
5. In the movie, a policeman's family is threatened by a **vindictive** former prisoner.		
6. The bullet **penetrate**d the wall of the room.		
7. I returned to my car in half an hour, and was **appall**ed to see the penalty notice on it.		
8. The artist is famous for his pictures of **voluptuous** women.		
9. In the medieval ages, knights displayed **dainty** handkerchiefs ladies gave to them.		
10. The **polarity** between the left and right wings of the party seems to be growing.		

語群①

（a）悪意に満ちた，（b）優美な，（c）脅威，（d）相違，（e）両極端，（f）官能的な，（g）強固にする，（h）擬似の，（i）貫く，（j）ぎょっとさせる

68

語群②

(ア) a difference, (イ) to enter something and pass through it, especially with force, (ウ) to make something stronger, (エ) expressing strong sexual feeling; sexually attractive, (オ) false or not real; imitating, (カ) unreasonably cruel and unfair towards someone, (キ) delicate, graceful and pretty, (ク) a state in which people, opinions, or ideas have opposite or contradictory aspects, (ケ) a person or thing that is dangerous, (コ) to make someone feel very shocked and upset

02 *Reading*

Finally, both stepsisters participate in a physical assault that **solidifi**es a hidden masculinity. Cinderella is dressed for the ball in a pink gown that her animal friends helped transform, while she finished the many chores expected of her by her stepfamily. (A) Realizing that the beautiful Cinderella will easily outshine her daughters, the music heightens ominously as Lady Tremaine helps her daughters notice that Cinderella's dress incorporated an abandoned sash and necklace, recently discarded from their closets. In what is arguably a **pseudo**-rape scene, Drizella first grabs and breaks Cinderella's necklace, while Anastasia pulls at Cinderella's dress. The stepsisters tear at the other girl's clothing, ripping it from her body while Cinderella attempts to shield herself, covering her neck, face, and body with her hands. Walt Disney described what he intended with the scene as "they rip the hell out of her.... As they're pulling the poor girl to pieces, the stepmother watches coldly with a little smile on her face." The dress is left as a one-shouldered rag, torn and ruined, and thus Cinderella cannot attend the ball. The stepsisters' angry, cruel faces loom large in the screen during the attack as their monstrous behavior confirms their lack of femininity.

In contrast to her flat-chested boyish daughters, Disney's Lady Tremaine manages to keep a vaguely female shape, but her facial features and behaviors mark her as both unfeminine as well as unmotherly, even to her own daughters. Her face is sharp-edged, with large eyes and a pointy chin, a clear **divergence** from Cinderella's softened cheeks, nose, and lips. Her nose is crooked and large for her face, more reminiscent of *101 Dalmatians* male villains Horace and Jasper, rather than typical Disney female features. (B)Her over-plucked, arched eyebrows characterize her expressions as surprised and menacing, while the coloring of her face, which transforms from gray and tan to dark green depending on her mood and actions, reveals the evilness associated with her. "There was hardly a moment when the Stepmother was not running something through her mind, constantly scheming, which made her such a **menace**. Her piercing, **penetrat**ing eyes gave a look of intense concentration as she watched Cinderella." With these physical characteristics a la Disney, Lady Tremaine is distanced from femininity.

(C)But it is her behavior to her daughters and stepdaughter that un-sexes her, as she dominates them thoroughly and harshly. While the tale always had her showing only cruelty to Cinderella, for no apparent reason, Disney's version takes the original and escalates it. Lady Tremaine trips the footman carrying the glass slipper in the original film—even though her own daughters' feet have already failed to fit it—so that Cinderella won't even have the opportunity to escape her tyranny. In *Cinderella III*, intent on gaining wealth and power, Lady Tremaine changes her own daughter's appearance into a copy of Cinderella via the magic wand so that Anastasia can marry the Prince. In perhaps the penultimate evil mother decision, she eventually attempts to kill Anastasia when the girl defies her mother. In a film series where ultra-feminine Cinderella sings even while doing an immense amount of unpleasant, never-ending chores, this **vindictive** villain's behavior pushes Lady Tremaine completely outside the realm of what Disney defines as feminine or motherly.

Ursula, the Sea Witch in *The Little Mermaid*, also retains some female qualities, but like Lady Tremaine, overwhelmingly communicates a transgendered presence. Ursula is a huge black and purple octopus, with styled white hair standing straight up, large eyes with deeply painted lids of blue and gray, and incredibly arched eyebrows. Her huge lips and nails are painted bright red, and she has a "beauty mark" mole on her right cheek. Her makeup, saggy jowls and large breasts create a vaguely female, **voluptuous** figure; however the exaggeration of those features, combined with her deep voice and overtly sexualized body movements suggests something much more masculinized. The Disney Villain remarks that "when we first see her in the film, we are **appall**ed at her appearance, and realize that here is someone to be reckoned with." Of course, the reason "we are appalled" is not just because this villain is scary (after all, the villains are supposed to be scary!). Instead audience members love (and hate) Ursula because she crosses gender boundaries and becomes a comic pseudo-female villain.

Physically, the sea-witch is drawn as a queer predatory monster with a grotesque overwhelming body that occupies the whole screen.... Moreover, Ursula's queerness subverts gender categories, thus turning this female witch into an ironic positive figure; "a multiple cross-dresser," who destabilises gender through her excess and theatricality.

When Ursula suggestively tells Ariel to use "body language" to attract Prince Eric, Ursula's overweight body and tentacles, her deep voice, and the excessive, sexualized shimmies are reminiscent of a drag queen on stage, overly made up and singing deeply, appearing both female and male simultaneously.

Some critics have argued that Ursula was always supposed to be transgendered; in fact, Pinsky notes Ursula "was modeled on the modern drag queen Divine, according to the film's directing animator, Reuben Acquino." Clearly with her white blond hair, overwhelming size, deepened voice, and accentuated eyebrows, the resemblance to Divine is uncanny. As well, many of her mannerisms and language choices also remind viewers of Divine. Complaining of her expulsion from King Triton's kingdom, Ursula exposes fleshy, wiggling upper arms, large rounded breasts over an excessive stomach, along with her sagging jowls, then says, "And now look at me—wasted away to practically nothing—banished and exiled and practically starving." The scene ends with her long thick black tentacles curling around the screen, until only her eyes are still apparent. Obviously this obese, overindulgent octopus is nowhere near malnourished, but the dramatic phrasing and movement coupled with her enormous size presents Ursula as overly theatrical and campy. Her exaggerated characteristics begin to read more and more like a flamboyant drag queen, than that of a real exile concerned with starvation.

In these ways, female villains become more and more separated from their **dainty** heroines, and their carefully-crafted creepiness depends on a distinct division from traditionally feminized characteristics (and the overtly heterosexual heroines mentioned earlier). As well, it's understandable that Disney would want the villains to appear distinctly different--their audience members are as young as one or two years old, and Disney wants the youngsters to identify with the heroes and heroines, clamoring for Disney Princess products after seeing each film. They need them to understand easily who is good and who is not—and they do, as shown by my daughter's comments and inclinations. But when Disney creates female villains primarily as transgendered characters--and transgendered characters as the primary evil characters in their storylines, then it crosses a line of attempting to show the **polarity** of good and evil to its youngsters, and becomes a disjointed misinformation telling young children that difference is not okay—in fact, that those who are transgendered are evil and to be avoided at all cost. These gross exaggerations and profiling create a disturbing message that is repeated ad nauseam to our youngest movie-watchers, who watch these films incessantly in our homes.

rip the hell out of　引き裂く。hell は強意語。
saggy　たるんだ。
jowls　あご。
predator　補食動物。
tentacle　触手。
shimmy　異常な振動。
Divine　ディヴァイン (1945~1988) アメリカの俳優。ドラァグ・クィーン姿で，『ピンク・フラミンゴ』(1972) などのカルト映画で活躍。
accentuate 強調する。
uncanny 薄気味悪い，奇怪な。
ad nauseam いやになる程。

03 Comprehension Questions

（A）次の文が本文の内容と一致する場合は T，一致しない場合は F を選びなさい。

① (T・F)	Cinderella's stepsisters prevented her from attending the ball with a pink gown that her animal friends made for her.
② (T・F)	Cinderella's stepmother doesn't act like a mother, not only to Cinderella but also to the heroine's stepsisters.
③ (T・F)	The appearance of Cinderella's stepmother is unfeminine like her real daughters.
④ (T・F)	Ursula in *The Little Mermaid* is different from Cinderella's stepsisters because she keeps a vaguely female shape.
⑤ (T・F)	The difference between female villains and traditionally feminized heroines has been growing in recent years.

（B）本文に関する次の問に答えましょう。

① What characteristics do Lady Tremaine in *Cinderella* and Ursula in *The Little Mermaid* have in common?

② What makes Lady Tremaine different from a traditional mother?

_____

③ What is the reason some critics claim that Ursula is transgendered?

_____

04 Grammatical Structure

本文中の下線 A，B，C の文の主節における主部と述部を見分けましょう。

	主部	述部
下線 A		
下線 B		
下線 C		

05 Summary

次の文中の（　　　）に本文から適語を選んで書き込みましょう。

　　When Lady Tremaine realizes that the beautiful Cinderella will easily outshine her daughters, she helps them notice that Cinderella's dress incorporated an abandoned sash and necklace, recently discarded from their closets. Her daughters (1.　　　　) Cinderella physically, which shows their (2.　　　　). On the other hand, while Lady Tremaine has a vaguely female shape, her (3.　　　) shows that she is not feminine nor (4.　　　　). Ursula in *The Little Mermaid* also has some female features but these are transgendered. This is supported by the fact that she looks similar to the modern drag queen Divine. Thus, Disney tries to make the villains to appear (5.　　　　) different from hero and heroines because their audience members are as young as one or two years old. They need them to understand easily who is good and who is not. But when Disney creates female villains primarily as transgendered characters, and transgendered characters as the primary evil characters in their storylines, then it goes beyond showing the (6.　　　　) of good and evil to its youngsters, and becomes a disjointed misinformation telling young children that difference is not all right and that those who are transgendered are evil and to be avoided at all cost. These (7.　　　) and profiling create a disturbing message that is repeated to our youngest movie-watchers, who watch these films incessantly in our homes.

06 Discussion/Writing/Presentation

次の問いかけについて，検討してみましょう。

① Show some examples of famous entertainers who are openly LGBT. What do you think of them?

② Compare villains in Disney movies and those in other movies in terms of their gender roles.

CHAPTER 14

Mean Ladies: Transgendered Villains in Disney Films (5)

00 Warm-up

映画『ライオン・キング／ *The Lion King*』(1994),『アラジン／ *Aladdin*』(1992),『ポカホンタス／ *Pocahontas*』(1995) の主要な登場人物と物語のあらすじを調べましょう。次に,「悪役」(villain) たちが, 作品中でどのような外見や話し方をしているかを自分なりに想像し, その特徴について, 英語で簡潔に発表しましょう。

01 Vocabulary

次の下線部の表現の意味を例文から推測し, 下欄の語群①から訳語を選びましょう。また, その言い換えとして最適な英語表現を下欄の語群②から選びましょう。

例文	語群①	語群②
1. At an early age she showed a great **aptitude** for music.		
2. We have to confront the **invidious** incivility of the new president.		
3. Turning around, Alice gave a perfect **curtsy** to the Queen of Hearts.		
4. At just five years of age Mary, Queen of Scots, was **betroth**ed to Henry VIII's son, Edward.		
5. The film director used music to **accentuate** the dramatic tension.		
6. The **preoccupation** with muscle building leads him to an endless quest to become bigger.		
7. The audition entries spend much time **preen**ing themselves in front of a mirror.		
8. It is claimed that **patriarchy** is a worldwide system which hinders the social progress of women and makes them dependent on men.		
9. The invention of the printing press became a great **incentive** to the development of literature		
10. He was teased at school because he spoke with a **lisp**.		

語群①

(a) ～を婚約させる, (b) 刺激・動機, (c) 適性・才能, (d) 舌足らずの発音, (e) ～を目立たせる, (f) 身づくろいをする, (g) しゃくにさわる, (h) 家父長制社会・男中心社会, (i) ひざを曲げるおじぎ, (j) 夢中にさせるもの

語群②

(ア) devote effort to making oneself look attractive and then admire one's appearance,
(イ) make more noticeable or prominent, (ウ) likely to arouse or incur resentment or anger
in others, (エ) a speech with imperfect articulation, (オ) formally engage someone to be
married, (カ) a social system in which men have all the power, (キ) the state or condition of being
preoccupied or engrossed with something, (ク) a natural ability to do something, (ケ) a thing that
motivates or encourages someone to do something, (コ) a woman's or girl's formal greeting made
by bending the knees with one foot in front of the other

02 Reading

Similarly fascinating (and equally problematic) is the way in which Disney's male villains are
crafted to avoid heterosexual competition with the heroes. By feminizing the male villain, even
bordering on overtly homosexual characterizations, *The Lion King*'s Scar, *Aladdin*'s Jafar, and
Pocahontas's Ratcliffe also become "mean ladies"—the stuff of which my daughter was wholly
terrified. But while they may be evil, they definitely aren't masculine.

(A)While the lion Scar looks only vaguely feminine in his appearance, his lack of physical
prowess, his language choices, and the lack of a female mate mark his character as crossing into
transgendered territory. Unlike the other two male lions (Mufasa and the adult Simba), Scar
willingly admits he has little physical **aptitude**, connecting him strangely with Disney's typical
portrayal of female characters. In one scene, Mufasa believes Scar has challenged him. Quickly
denying being insolent to the much-fiercer Mufasa, Scar continues "Well, as far as brains go, I got
the lion's share. But, when it comes to brute strength ... I'm afraid I'm at the shallow end of the gene
pool." Sean Griffin states in *Tinker Belles and Evil Queens: The Walt Disney Company from the
Inside* Out that Scar "makes up for his lack of strength with catty remarks and **invidious** plotting ...
fairly swish[ing] ... in his attempt to usurp the throne." Scar uses his body and his tone, much like
Ursula did, to carefully craft his transgenderism.

Later, another sarcastic reply again promotes the idea of Scar as transgendered. Noticing Scar's
continued lack of respect for the future ascension, Mufasa points out his son Simba will be king.
(B)Scar's sardonic "I'll practice my **curtsy**" reiterates his acerbic personality, but also adds a
transgendered effect as it locates Scar again in the female role, curtsying instead of bowing to the
future king. Like Drizella's bow to the Prince, the gendered behavior reversal draws the attention of
the viewer, categorizing Scar as gender-bending.

Scar also has no mate, even when he becomes King. (C)Unlike Mufasa, who mated with Sarabi,
and Simba who is **betroth**ed to Nala, Scar chooses no lioness as his queen, and thus, has no heir.
He depends on Sarabi for her food gathering skills, even though they share no romantic interest. In
fact, Scar's main friends are outside the pride as he bullies and rules the hyena pack, marking him
as living far outside the heterosexist lion culture. Feminized and powerless, Scar cannot compete
with his brother or nephew, even though he targets them as rivals. Just as when preschool viewers
knew that Anastasia wasn't a true princess (even though the shoe fit), they likewise realize that Scar
isn't the true king—his covert homosexual status helps them know he's the bad guy.

Jafar, as the male villain in *Aladdin*, also crosses gender boundaries via appearance and behavior. Tall and thin, Jafar's posture and bearing **accentuate**s his difference from other male characters. As Li-Vollmer and LaPointe note, "Jafar ... wears a long gown with a nipped waist and sleeves that billow above the elbow and fit closely along the forearm to reveal his very slender lower arms and wrists. The pronounced ornamentation on the shoulders of his gown only direct more attention to the artifice of broad shoulders, not the true broad physique of a real man. All the other men, including the Sultan and other high-ranking characters, wear pants." Likewise, Jafar is the only male in the film to wear eye make-up, typically a female **preoccupation**. Again, Li-Vollmer and LaPointe observe "These cosmetic forms of gender transgression are most noticeable in the context of other male characters, whose facial features are not highlighted with animators' cosmetics." Subtly differentiating male villains from the male heroes via makeup and costume, the bad guys are increasingly associated with femaleness. Li-Vollmer and LaPoint also observe that several male Disney Villains "have ... tall, willowy frames with gracefully slender limbs and slim waists," which are strangely close to our original "mean ladies"—the evil queen in *Snow White* and Maleficent in *Sleeping Beauty*.

Additionally, Jafar's behavior is feminized. He is prissy and **preen**ing, unwilling to explore The Cave of Wonders for the magic lantern himself (unlike the heroes and heroines who eagerly head into adventurous escapades, even if they are dangerous). Sean Griffin also shares that lead animator Andreas Deja "admits to conceiving of the [Jafar] character as a gay man 'to give him his theatrical quality, his elegance.'" Griffin continues, arguing it is easy to find the "'gay-tinged' villainy in Disney ... by watching how Jafar arches his eyebrows in disdain, or in the sneer that curls Scar's mouth as he endures the heterosexual **patriarchy** in which he finds himself."

Like Scar, Jafar's lack of interest in a female partner also suggests his transgenderism. Jafar shows no romantic or sexual interest in the beautiful Jasmine until his male sidekick, Iago, suggests marrying Jasmine in order to become Sultan; and when Jafar does force Jasmine to obey him (wishing the Genie to compel her to fall in love with him), the wish is not motivated by lust, but rather by his obsession for more power. Thus, Jafar's only **incentive** to pursue a heterosexual relationship is to humiliate Jasmine and anger Aladdin.

However, the male villain in *Pocahontas* exhibits the most flamboyantly transgendered characteristics of all male Disney villains. Governor John Ratcliffe first appears on screen dressed in pink and purple clothes, sporting pigtails tied with pink bows, and carrying a small lapdog. He puts his pinky finger up to drink his tea and dances effeminately, wearing a pink feathered boa. David Ogden Stiers affects a **lisp** in the voice for Ratcliffe, contributing to the stereotypical homosexual model. Ratcliffe's associates are also affected by his transgendered depiction: his pug is shown with a bouffant hairdo in a bubble bath, while Ratcliffe's male manservant, Wiggins, speaks with a high-pitched voice, cuts topiary into animal shapes, and desires to create gift baskets for the Indians. Clearly, Ratcliffe is not the masculinized hero like John Smith, nor the serious Indian warrior, Koucom. Instead he is the unlikable villain, who is yet another "mean lady": effete, if not outright homosexual.

lion's share　ライオンの分け前，最大の分け前。
catty　コソコソした，意地悪な。
swish　「女性的な男性同性愛者」を意味する米俗語表現。形容詞として使う場合は，「(男が)女のような」の意。英俗語では「しゃれた」「スマートな」の意もある。
prissy　口やかましい。
pinky finger　小指。
pigtail　（女の子が髪を編んで，後ろに垂らす）おさげ。

boa 襟巻き。
pug パグ（犬）。
bouffant ふっくらした。
topiary 装飾的に刈り込んだ。
John Smith ジョン・スミス **(1580~1631)** イギリスの軍人。『ポカホンタス』に登場する。
effete 精力の尽きた。
Maleficent マレフィセント。『眠れる森の美女』に登場する悪役。アンジェリナ・ジョリーが主演した『マレフィセント』
(2014) では、彼女の視点から『眠れる森の美女』が描かれる。フェミニズム的リメイクとなっている。

03 *Comprehension Questions*

（A）次の文が本文の内容と一致する場合は T，一致しない場合は F を選びなさい。

① (T・F)	Because of their lack of masculine characteristics, Scar, Jafar and Ratcliffe are equivalent to "mean ladies."
② (T・F)	Scar's gender transgression is emphasized by his way of greeting the future king.
③ (T・F)	Children easily recognize Scar as a villain by his competitiveness with his rivals.
④ (T・F)	According to Sean Griffin, some male villains in Disney are given particular facial movements to make them heterosexual.
⑤ (T・F)	The pompous hairstyle of Ratcliffe's dog and the bass voice of the male servant are associated with their master's effeminacy.

（B）本文に関する次の問に答えましょう。

① According to Sean Griffin, how does Scar compensate for his physical inferiority in order to claim the throne?

_____

② According to Li-Vollmer and LaPointe, what does the decoration on the shoulders of Jafar's gown accentuate?

_____

③ How does David Ogden Stiers conduce to the establishment of the homosexual stereotype?

_____

04 *Grammatical Structure*

本文中の下線 A，B，C の文の主節における主部と述部を見分けましょう。

	主部	述部
下線 A		
下線 B		
下線 C		

05 Summary

次の文中の（　　　）に本文から適語を選んで書き込みましょう。

It is interesting and problematic also to see the way Disney makes a male villain look like a typical female character. *The Lion King*'s Scar, *Aladdin*'s Jafar, and *Pocahontas*'s Ratcliffe are all feminized, which prompts children to recognize they are evil because they are not (1.　　　　　). Scar is deprived of masculinity by his lack of physical prowess and by his feminine behaviors, like (2.　　　　) instead of bowing. The lack of a female partner also suggests his transgenderism. Jafar also crosses gender boundaries by his appearance and behavior. He wears a long, colorful (3.　　　　), for example, to accentuate his femininity. Also, he is the only male in the film to put on (4.　　　　), which is a typical female preoccupation. His feminine behavior and gestures also emphasize his derailing from traditional gender norms, so it is easy to find "gay" attributes in him as Sean Griffin argues. Furthermore, Ratcliffe is the most flamboyantly transgendered character of all male villains. His gaudy clothes of pink and purple and his effeminate behavior draw attention to his transgenderism. The (5.　　　　) actor adopts a lisp for the character, to make him appear to be homosexual. Therefore, these three male villains are "mean (6.　　　　)," the typical portrayal of female villains in Disney, which tells the child (7.　　　　) that people with transgendered appearance are bad guys.

06 Discussion/Writing/Presentation

次の問いかけについて，検討してみましょう。

① Do you think our idea of masculinity and femininity is affected by the movies we see in our childhood?

② Do you think wearing makeup or flamboyant costumes are feminine preoccupations?

CHAPTER 15

Mean Ladies: Transgendered Villains in Disney Films (6)

00 Warm-up

子供の頃の自分に女らしさや男らしさのイメージを与えた映画についてクラスメートと話し合いましょう。また，ディズニー映画のヒーロー，ヒロイン，悪役たちが子供たちにどのような影響を与え得るかについて，具体的な登場人物を挙げて自分の考えを英語で説明しましょう。その際には，PowerPoint などを用いてわかりやすい発表を目指しましょう。

01 Vocabulary

次の下線部の表現の意味を例文から推測し，下欄の語群①から訳語を選びましょう。また，その言い換えとして最適な英語表現を下欄の語群②から選びましょう。

例文	語群①	語群②
1. The volunteers **partake** in fundraising for donations.		
2. The Nobel Peace Prize was awarded to ICAN which urged world leaders to **eliminate** nuclear weapons.		
3. Being blinded by the power of money, he **disassociate**d from his political convictions.		
4. They held hands together and disappeared from a world **soak**ed in hatred.		
5. The diplomat denied that he was a racist, after his vulgar **disparagement** of African countries.		
6. The professor's newly-published book is about the Nazis' **homophobia** and their destruction of the German gay-rights movement.		
7. The experts have warned that the new system could leave the users **vulnerable** to cyber attacks.		
8. It is imperative to observe children's play in order to understand how kids develop their **schema**ta.		
9. Our boss is **susceptible** to women who cry.		
10. The government bureaucrat has been accused of falsifying the document and telling **despicable** lies.		

語群①

(a) 感じやすい・影響を受けやすい，(b) スキーマ（知識を体制化する心的な枠組み），
(c) 加わる，(d) 卑劣な，(e) 絶交する・つきあいをやめる，(f) 除去する，(g) おとしめ
ること・軽蔑，(h) 満ちている・浸す，(i) 同性愛嫌悪，(j) 脆弱な・冒されやすい

語群②

（ア）dislike of or prejudice against homosexual people，（イ）to completely remove or get rid of，
（ウ）easily hurt, influenced, or attacked; exposed to the possibility of being harmed either physically
or emotionally，（エ）a pattern of thought or behavior that organizes categories of information and
the relationships among them，（オ）take part in an activity or event，（カ）deserving hatred and
contempt，（キ）to become saturated; to permeate thoroughly as liquid does，（ク）likely or liable to
be easily influenced or affected by a particular thing，（ケ）to disconnect or separate，（コ）the act of
regarding or representing something as being of little worth

02 Reading

By reinforcing the gender-bending identity of Ratcliffe in contrast to the heterosexual male characters, Ratcliffe becomes more unpleasant, more untouchable, and more remote. Sassafras Lowrey adds that Ratcliffe does not **partake** in the physical work of "digging up Virginia" ... he dresse[s] flamboyantly and sings "I'll glitter," positioning him far outside of the norms of acceptable heterosexual masculinity. This is particularly true as men who are performing physical labor, thus displaying stereotypical heterosexual actions[,] surround him.

In fact, *The Disney Villain* states clearly that the animators "preferred to depict our examples of vileness through a strong design which **eliminate**d realism and kept the audience from getting too close to the character." (A)While this statement refers to the "safe distance" kept between the devil via his screen positioning, for example, in *Fantasia*, and viewers, it can also refer to the distance created via villains who appear different from the preschool viewer. In other words, child viewers understand that not only is Ratcliffe the villain, but he is the gay villain who is clearly different from almost every other male character in the film. (B)By making him grossly flamboyant and disparate from all other men, while associating him with greed, violence, and ignorance, child viewers **disassociate** completely from his character, glad that he ends up in the brig on the way home. This breeds blatant prejudices among children viewers regarding any difference, but especially those which are associated with transgenderism.

Disney films are often regarded as harmless family entertainment—one in which members of all ages are welcome to enjoy the thrills and spills of their favorite animated character. As such, they have been overlooked until recently as content in need of analysis. The transgendered villains and their hyper-heterosexual heroes and heroines offer an interesting contrast to each other worth exploring more deeply, as does the problematic message about gender and difference that is being sent consistently to Disney's child viewers.

While there are no Disney characters that actively announce their homosexuality or transgenderism, there is considerable evidence that Disney's gender-bending characters are flourishing. Fascinatingly, some of these transgendered characters are among the most popular. Ursula and Scar consistently rank highly, not just among villains, but also among all Disney characters. So then, if some of these transgendered characters still manage to gain a following, why is it significant to note this strangely fascinating pattern?

Obviously Disney is a powerhouse media outlet, watched by millions of children all over the world, and "the Disney Princess films comprise five of the six top revenue-generating Disney films of all time." It has been argued by H.A. Giroux that Disney films influence children as much as other cultural influences, such as school, church, and family, as their videos are repetitively watched via home DVDs. Thus, the characterization of transgendered villains marks gender-bending characters (and eventually real people) as "evil" simply through the ongoing establishment of the pattern; i.e., if the "mean ladies" are consistently transgendered, it implies a larger statement is being made about what kind of people cross traditional gender boundaries in behavior and appearance—and that larger statement is one **soak**ed in prejudice and **disparagement**.

(C)Finally, creating only villains as transgendered people also suggests something about the consumerism of these films—i.e., that Disney willingly plays into stereotypes and fears about **homophobia** as well as accepts the crushing dominance of heterosexism within the larger community. In other words, if all of the villains are gay or have complicated gender-bending identities, it suggests that viewers find homosexuality or untraditional gender behavior and appearance unsettling, at best, and thus, that it's okay to treat people who are different from the heterosexual norm as dangerous or disgusting because they will hurt you; after all, they are villains. At worst, viewers may feel they can be openly hostile to those who are different via transgendered appearance and behavior—and our preschool set is especially **vulnerable** to this message. As Li-Vollmer and LaPointe argue,

By drawing on information gleaned from their real-life encounters and their viewing of media images, children organize information about gender roles and gender performances into their schemata about what it is to be male or female (Fiske & Taylor, 1991); therefore, media viewing is both a source and a location of children's gender **schema** development (Durkin, 1984). Children's gender schemata, like all schemata, are less developed than those of adults, and are, therefore, more **susceptible** to influence from new sources and experiences, including media; as young people's gender schemata develop over time, they become more resilient to change (Fiske & Taylor, 1991).

So, when my daughter asks me at the grocery store if the cashier is a boy or a girl, because he has a ponytail, I have to realize that she's responding to the abundance of traditional gendered stereotypes in our culture, including confusing signals from Disney films—and she's right, most boys don't wear ponytails; longer hair and ponytails can be characteristics that are associated with girls. However, since some boys wear ponytails (and some girls don short-clipped hair), it's also important to explain that the gendered difference she's noting on the outside is only part of the picture, and it may have little to do with behavior or intent. The ponytail-wearing man is not evil simply because he challenges a gendered stereotype. Thus, while the Disney villains are mean, cruel, and petty, often out to rule the world in **despicable** ways, it's not because they are girly men or tomboys.

Fantasia 『ファンタジア』　1940 年のディズニー・アニメーション。アニメとクラシック音楽を結びつけ，芸術度の高いものとなった。
brig　刑務所。
blatant　露骨な。
thrills and spills　エキサイティングなイベント。
schemata　schema の複数形　スキーマ，図式。
tomboy　おてんば。

03 *Comprehension Questions*

（A）次の文が本文の内容と一致する場合は T，一致しない場合は F を選びなさい。

① (T・F)	According to *The Disney Villain*, the animators design villains who are too realistic to arouse the viewer's compassionate feelings.
② (T・F)	Making Ratcliffe vile and different from other male characters creates a hotbed of prejudice among child viewers.
③ (T・F)	There have not been sufficient analyses until recently about how harmless Disney films may be for child viewers.
④ (T・F)	Disney's villains outside of the heterosexual norm may cause the viewers to feel uncomfortable and even be aggressive towards transgendered people.
⑤ (T・F)	LiVollmer and LaPointe suggest that children are easily affected by the media because their gender schemata become flexible as they grow.

（B）本文に関する次の問に答えましょう。

① According to H. A. Giroux, why do Disney films have a significant influence on children?

_____

② What are the problems with creating only villains as transgendered people?

_____

③ What does the author think we should recognize when girls don't feel right with boys wearing ponytails?

_____

04 *Grammatical Structure*

本文中の下線 A，B，C の文の主節における主部と述部を見分けましょう。

	主部	述部
下線 A		
下線 B		
下線 C		

05 Summary

次の文中の（　　　）に本文から適語を選んで書き込みましょう。

　By portraying the villains in a less realistic way, Disney animators create a safe (1.　　　　　) between the audience and the villains, and, consequently, make child viewers feel distant from them. Children, thus, understand that the character who looks different from other male characters is a bad guy. This nurtures (2.　　　　　) among children against transgenderism. Creating only (3.　　　　　) as transgendered people champions heterosexism and accelerates homophobia, making people feel homosexuality or transgenderism is disgusting, and even pushing them to be (4.　　　　　) to transgendered people. As researchers argue, children are vulnerable to messages from the media because their (5.　　　　　) are less developed than those of adults. This is why it is problematical to regard Disney films just as harmless family entertainment. Disney is such a powerful medium, which influences children as much as other cultural influences, that associating the characters' transgendered appearance and behavior with evilness exposes people who cross the traditional gender boundaries to prejudice and (6.　　　　　). Therefore, we know how much children are affected by the cultural gendered stereotypes given by powerful media like Disney films, when we see them feel confused by boys with long hair and ponytails. It is important to tell children that people portrayed as girly men or tomboys are not villains but ones who (7.　　　　　) a gendered stereotype.

06 Discussion/Writing/Presentation

次の問いかけについて，検討してみましょう。

① Do you think media like TV or movies may promote prejudices against LGBT people?

② Do you think Japanese entertainment media including animations and television dramas may persuade us that the heterosexual lifestyle is the best choice of life?

音声ファイルのダウンロード方法

英宝社ホームページ（http://www.eihosha.co.jp/）の
「テキスト音声ダウンロード」バナーをクリックすると、
音声ファイルダウンロードページにアクセスできます。

Disney Films and Secret Messages
Race, Ethnicity, Gender and Sexuality
ディズニーアニメと多様化する社会

2019年1月15日　初　版　　　2022年2月10日　第3刷

著　者　　國友 万裕　　安田 優
　　　　　松本 恵美　井上 裕子　長岡 亜生　轟 里香
　　　　　村上 裕美　船本 弘史　須田 久美子

発 行 者　　佐々木　元

発 行 所　株式会社　英　宝　社
　　　　　〒101-0032 東京都千代田区岩本町 2-7-7
　　　　　TEL 03 (5833) 5870-1　FAX 03 (5833) 5872

製版・表紙デザイン：伊谷企画／印刷・製本：日本ハイコム株式会社
ISBN 978-4-269-11008-3 C1082

本テキストの一部または全部を、コピー、スキャン、デジ
タル化等での無断複写・複製は、著作権法上での例外
を除き禁じられています。本テキストを代行業者等の第
三者に依頼してのスキャンやデジタル化はたとえ個人や家
庭内での利用であっても著作権侵害となり、著作権法上
一切認められておりません。